MW01537686

1

"Yeah, I'm an open book."

Amy Winehouse

First printing

ISBN: 978-1463779870
Published By: Neptunes Publishing

www.neptunespublishing.com
Printed in the United States of America
Poisoning Sylvie is printed in Helvetica World

Andy Morris*:* I dedicate this book to my beautiful daughter Ella, so cruelly ripped from my life in May 2009. One day she will read this book and know how much I love her, how much I yearn for her every day.

Christina Westover*:* I would like to thank Andy, Hollace M. Metzger and Ren Garcia for their continued support and inspiration. Thank you from the bottom of my heart.

Five stolen months.

She looked into my eyes

Straight into her own eyes.

And she knew.

Not even an hour later, a woman with a kind face and a cool heart said "time's up."

My baby kissed me the fourth week.

Next week, ran to me with arms spread high and wide.

Will she ever understand

How we were born on the same day?

I for the second time.

(from "Father and daughter" by Andy Dene Morris)

Open Book:
The Life and Death
Of Amy Winehouse

Andy Morris &
Christina Westover

Published by Neptunes Publishing

Table Of Contents

INTRODUCTION

Like many Americans, my first glimpse of Amy Winehouse was her 2007 appearance on Late Night With David Letterman.

Of course, I had heard the song "Rehab" with its catchy chorus sung to a blues jazz tune, and a drum beat as modern as her pierced lip. I was familiar enough with the song that I often caught myself singing it, or tapping my feet to the music which played in my head.

I was a fan of Amy Winehouse's work without knowing anything about her, which is why I was thrilled to hear she would be performing on the show.
Before seeing her on Late Night With David Letterman, I had no preconceived notions about what Amy Winehouse looked like, dressed like, or how she behaved. I only knew two things about her—first, that she had an amazing voice, and second, that she was black.

I couldn't have been more wrong. With her hair styled in a beehive and wearing a black fifties styled dress which exposed her tattoos, her raven-black hair was a screaming contrast to her fair skin. Her stage presence could not have been more magnetic.

The moment she began to sing I was mesmerized and intrigued. Performing on the screen was one of the most contradictory individuals I had ever seen. A young woman with the voice of an old soul. An old-fashioned sense of style presented in a modern hipster way. A singer whose polished demeanor belied the rebelliousness evident in her lyrics. The unpredictability and diversity of Amy Winehouse was delightful.

Having tremendous vocal range and the gift of melodic rhythm, Amy called herself a "black girl in a white girl's body."

She was not just a singer, but gifted songwriter whose intuitive lyrics and memorable hooks brought her world-wide acclaim.

As much as she prided herself on not caring what others thought of her for being different, a part of her still longed to be recognized and appreciated for her art.

She once commented on how jazz artists are taken seriously and treated with respect in a way many other musicians are not, and how she wanted to be recognized on the level of a jazz musician. She scoffed at the music played by most radio stations, calling it "watered down."

A visionary with fathomless depth and insatiable passion, she was a singer who wrote the songs she wanted to hear—songs which catapulted her career making her the first British female to ever win five Grammy Awards.

Despite her fame and success, Amy Winehouse suffered from depression, was even diagnosed as manic-depressive. Whether her increasing drug addictions were a result of self-medicating due to her depression can only be speculated.

Failed attempts at rehab and an ever growing drug addiction chronicled in media reports pictured the sharp decline of a once vibrant young woman whose voice and music were a gift to the world. "I'm an open book," Amy once said. Drunken bouts, physical assaults, arrests, even smoking drugs while walking the streets of London, Amy's spiraling health was recorded for the world to witness.

As destructive as she continued to be, the public displayed their grief and shock at the announcement of her death on July 23, 2011. Another young musician whose death added her to the list of the 27 Club—a list including Jim Morrison, Jimi Hendrix, Janis Joplin, and Kurt Cobain all who died at age 27.

Drugs, sex and rock and roll. Bisexuality, rehab, and a voice as hot as the sun. Amy Winehouse was a dreamer and idealist who proved to the world that embracing one's differences will always find a common ground in art, and that those who do not sell-out are those who do not fade.

Unique, fierce and inspiring, Amy Winehouse will never be forgotten.

Christina Westover

EARLY LIFE

To her mother, Janis, Amy Winehouse was a problem even before she was born.

The woman who would later have to resort to writing a letter to her troubled daughter via a British newspaper, to try and get her to change her ways and come home, had had a relatively easy time with her first child.

Alex Winehouse was born in 1979, with Janis interrupting her career as a pharmacy technician to take care of him while her husband Mitch brought the money into the house from his work as a window salesman.

The Winehouse home was a happy one, often filled with music as Mitch loved jazz and Janis, born and raised in Brooklyn, enjoyed playing her favorite US singer-songwriter records, especially James Taylor and Carole King.

Janis, though, had suffered periodic bouts of a mystery illness and when she fell pregnant with her second child in early 1983, the symptoms worsened.

She was struck by a strange prickling sensation running up and down her limbs, coupled with an overwhelming tiredness.

Janis dismissed it as "just pins and needles" and in the weeks after the birth of Amy in September 1983 decided the tiredness must be down to sleepless nights with the new baby.

In fact, many years would go by before Janis' illness was finally diagnosed. She suffered a total collapse, and tests showed she was suffering from multiple sclerosis. Her illness goes a long way to explaining why she felt unable to take a leading role in taming her daughter.

Even as a small child, Amy had been a worry for her parents – one time she almost choked to death on some cellophane. She would also pretend to be choking or, when she was old enough to be out by herself, deliberately go missing in a shopping centre, said Mitch. "What she really likes is for people to worry about her," he said.

North London is an area with a large Jewish population, so the Winehouses were at home in the suburb of Southgate.

Rather than being a religious home, it was one with music at the centre. A home where a young Amy would have been encouraged to express her emotions through artistic mediums. From an early age, Amy's creative drive was evident. She was confident in her abilities, and always intuitively knew what others would like because she most likely knew what interested her on layered levels.

Two of Amy's uncles are professional jazz musicians, and her father Mitch always had a good singing voice – much later, he signed to a recording label. He would hold young Amy rapt with his versions of Frank Sinatra's songs.

Amy was encouraged to sing, too, and was not to be discouraged from this once she started school. Teachers found it difficult to keep her quiet in class as she wanted to keep singing.

Amy couldn't understand what the problem was. As far as she was concerned, she wasn't misbehaving. She later said: "I was a good girl, I really liked school. I really liked learning. I wasn't really a trouble-maker you know... not more than other kids.

"I've always sung. I always assumed that everyone could sing, that that's what they do when they're happy or sad."

Janis encouraged both her children at their studies. She had taken an Open University science degree, then studied at the London School of Pharmacy, and her career success had seen the family move from a cramped two-bedroom apartment, and eventually a pretty three-bedroom Victorian town house.

She told the *Daily Mail* newspaper: "Amy was a beautiful child, always busy, always curious.

"She was always very cheery but she was also shy. She's never been an easy child."

Mitch told *Rolling Stone*: "She was always very self-willed. Not badly behaved but...different."

Amy was close to her father, and later would have "Daddy's Girl" tattooed on her shoulder, but the family's happiness was put under strain by the amount of time Mitch spent on the road with his job.

He met a woman, Jane, and began a long-term affair which he confessed to Janis.

"I think Mitchell would have liked to have both of us but I wasn't happy to do that," she later recalled.

"People talk a lot about the anger in Amy's songs. I think a lot of it was that her father wasn't there."

The Winehouses were to split when Amy was nine.

Mitch later acknowledged that his walking out affected both Amy and Alex, even though ironically they were to see more of him.

He said: "In the end, they said, 'Dad, you really don't have to come here every day!' But I couldn't be without them. I had to see them every day – which was causing Janis problems. But, obviously, when I left home I was guilt-ridden; not because of Janis, but because of the children. Although it was definitely the right thing to do."

However, Mitch's cheating and betrayal of trust would always haunt Amy. She would forever seek solace from the men who could nurture her the way Mitch did. The only problem was, they often shared her self-destructive tendencies, and because she had a tendency to lose herself in her lovers, she often could not separate herself from them during destructive rampages.

It must have upset her at the time, and her behavior at Osidge Primary School began to suffer.

Amy was to revisit the school some years later, for a photo shoot once she had established herself as a star. It was not a happy return.

She recalled: "My old teacher was there - this cold blooded bitch, she bleeds ice. She's had the same haircut since 1840.

"I was there with my friend and after the shoot we were like, 'Miss, hello Miss, can we have a look round the school?' "She was like, grudgingly, 'OK' and we went to the art room and my friend wandered off.

"Next thing, he shouted, 'Run! I've smashed the fire alarm!' and the whole school was evacuated. "It was the highlight of my life. I was saying, 'I do hope it's just a drill, Miss,' and her face was a picture."

Amy had a wonderful sense of humor. She was bold and sarcastic, with a gift for saying the right thing at the right moment for greater impact.

It was only years later she felt able to analyse the family dynamic, and look back on her parents' divorce as a positive thing.

She said: "Me and my Dad are two peas in a pod. We're really impulsive people. It's good that my Dad moved out when I was growing up, or we would have had some terrible clashes."

Though the separation was amicable, Amy sought refuge in the company of her grandmother, Cynthia, who lived just down the road.

Cynthia made sure she was in the audience for all of Amy's frequent appearances in school plays, and it was her suggestion that she enrol at the Susi Earnshaw Theatre School.

Based in nearby Barnet, the Susi Earnshaw is a full-time private school specialising in performing arts. Its reputation had been growing since it was founded in 1989 by Susi, a former actress, and her producer husband David.

David, who was the school's principal, had also been a session musician and encouraged the pupils to develop their singing abilities.

Young Amy needed little prompting, and at the age of 10 formed a rap group with best friend Juliette Ashby.

Amy and Juliette had known each other since they were both four, and used to egg each other on with dares. The singer later recalled that they had told a boy in school they wouldn't be friends with him anymore, unless he pulled down his pants. Which he did, said Juliette, and "that was when we truly bonded."

She added: "One of our best routines was that one of us would run out of the classroom in tears, and the other would say that they'd have to go out and comfort her. And then we'd just sit in a room somewhere, laughing for the rest of the lesson."

The pair were big fans of rappers Salt-N-Pepa, who had had a big hit with "Push It", and called their own group Sweet 'n Sour.

"I was Sour, of course," she recalled. "We had a tune called 'Spinderella', which was great."

'Spinderella' showed on many levels that Amy was organized, focused, creatively driven, and confident enough in her abilities that she was willing to go public with her work. It was an important moment—a time when she perhaps realized not only what it would take to be a singer/songwriter, but that she was completely capable of accomplishing this. Defining moments such as this were whispers of the world-wide fame to come.

The duo was short-lived, but her first taste of being a singer-songwriter was to prove more than a passing fancy.

At one time, she had dreams of becoming a roller-skating waitress, but from now on she began to dream of a recording career.

Janis recalled: "My mother-in-law and I took the kids to Cyprus on holiday. There was a talent show and she really wanted to enter it.

"She did and we sat there listening to her and I think that's when I knew that she had something really special."

Mitch, too, was blown away when he saw her on stage. He would later recall that, the first time he heard her sing in a school show, he had turned to Janis and said: "Thank God she can act and dance, 'cause she can't sing."

His familiarity with jazz meant he could see where, at times, her basic technique was lacking. On one occasion he helped her prepare for an audition, where she was to sing "Sunny Side of the Street." He recalled: "She couldn't quite get it right, and I said, 'Right, let's concentrate on your breathing, we'll listen to the record, listen to where Ella Fitzgerald takes a breath and work it out.'"

All the same, the way she was able to develop at a tender age and belt out a tune on stage was to blow him away. "I went to see her in a recital and I thought she'd just be acting," he said. "But then she came out on the stage and started singing, and I couldn't believe it. I never knew she could sing like that."

It was becoming evident to all watching that Amy's interest in music went far deeper than the desire to earn money. She had a pure love for music and song, and a sincere desire to share her voice which was her instrument of choice.

After four years at the Earnshaw school, she set her sights on attending the Sylvia Youth Theatre School. She organised an interview for herself, and won a place.

Puberty, though, brought the first signs of open rebellion from Amy as she flouted school rules by piercing her nose.

That did little to endear her to the principal, but it was her lack of academic success which was her big downfall as far as he was concerned.

Janis said: "The principal phoned up and asked me to come in and see him. He said, 'I think you should take her away.'

"He didn't want children who weren't going to get good grades and Amy wasn't going to."

She may have only attended the institution for a short while, but her reputation spread among her fellow students.

Mcfly star Tom Fletcher was a contemporary of hers. He later recalled: "She was a few years older than me when we were at Sylvia Young, so I wasn't friends (with her) or anything but it is quite a small school so everybody knows each other.

"She wasn't in many of my classes but she had a reputation back then of being quite wild. (But) I knew that she was extremely talented and she had an amazing voice."

Amy admitted years later she had been "devastated" to leave the Sylvia Young School, as she was happy there.

She said: "They've got a reputation because they are the best. It's not a pop star factory, they channel your creativity and you learn to use it. That's what I did. For every precocious kid there were kids who really worked. They sent you out to work. Stage school is a job. You learn how to get the fuck on with it. I learned a lot of important things."

Janis was disappointed at being asked to take Amy out of the Sylvia Young school, but could understand the principal's viewpoint. "She was very bright, but she was always messing around," she told the *Daily Mail*.

She found Amy a place at The Mount, an independent girls' school in the suburb of Mill Hill. No sooner had she moved schools than she began to push the boundaries with her parents, especially her mother, with whom she lived for most of the time. Aged 15, she got her first tattoo – a small Betty Boop on her back.

She was to tell Rolling Stone that, at that point, "My parents pretty much realized I would do whatever I wanted, and that was it, really."

HER CAREER BEGINS

Though her relationships with men were to be largely negative, Amy Winehouse's first real boyfriend played a significant part in launching her career.

Inspired by her enjoyment of writing her first songs with Sweet 'n Sour, Amy started learning guitar at the age of 13. At first she borrowed Alex's guitar, then she got her own as a present and began writing songs on it while imagining that she was playing on stage in front of Tony Bennett.

Aged 15, she started met soul singer Tyler James. The pair began dating, and James helped her first put together a demo tape, then sent it off to several companies' A&R departments.

At the same time, she was developing her performing style by playing in local pubs.

Her first songs, influenced by what she was listening to at the time, were rap.

But she had always had eclectic tastes, as she later recalled.

"I've listened to a lot of different things," she said. "I mean I learnt to sing from Dinah Washington and Sarah Vaughan, Minnie Ripperton… and my brother liked listening to all this stuff that I really learnt from. You don't necessarily learn to sing from singers, you learn from soloists as well. I like singers like Billie Holiday and Ella Fitzgerald."

She added: "From the age of 11 I was listening to Ella, who would sing the song perfectly but in a straight way, and then I learnt about subtlety. I heard people like Sarah Vaughan use her voice as an instrument, and that inspired me so much because it made me realize that a whisper can be so much more effective than just belting something out."

Though she said she was not too ambitious at first, she didn't lack balls when it came to playing in front of a crowd.

She said: "I really didn't start knocking on management company doors or anything. I wrote some songs, started playing gigs.

"I just played pub gigs. I had some songs and just did pub gigs. I'd go in with my Strat or something and just play pub gigs. I used to do gigs with a band called the Bolsha Band.

"It was cool because if they were playing they'd have their ramp there and I could go on before them, do a few songs... like just me... and then they'd do their set... I'd then go and do a couple of songs with them at the end of their set."

The Bolsha Band were not destined to set the music charts alight, but it was not long before Amy's reputation had spread as far as Simon Fuller.

A former Chrysalis executive, who had signed Madonna to the label back in 1983, Fuller founded his own management company 19 Entertainment two years later. The name came from the anti-war song "19" by Paul Hardcastle, which had been a No.1 on both sides of the Atlantic thanks to Fuller's promotional skills.

By 2000, Fuller had branched out into TV and founded the Idol franchise, which now reaches more than 100 countries. But his management company continued to flourish as he signed up the likes of David and Victoria Beckham and the Spice Girls.

Fuller wanted to sign Amy, and approached Janis. She recalled: "We had a meeting with the company because she was still so young they needed our consent to manage her.

"I wanted her to stay on at school but she said, 'No, this is what I really want.' I think she was too young and thereby hangs the tale."

Though he was confident of her talent, Fuller decided to keep his new signing under wraps for a while.

Amy was to later insist she had only met Fuller twice during her time with his company. And she was not afraid to bite the hand that feeds, when talking about him to the press.

She told one interviewer: "I'll tell you what people should worry about. The fact that Simon, when S Club started fucking up ... he replaced them. SClub 7, SClub 8 ... it's all the same. Now that's fucked. He's mad, that Simon Fuller."

She added: "I don't think he cares if he gets a return on me. He's got Pop Idol and his empire. He's a smart man, and he's clever enough to know he can't fuck with me."

Her future A&R representative at Island/Universal, Darcus Beese, later told how he had been frustrated, after first hearing Amy sing. He decided right then that he wanted to work with her, but it was not that simple.

He told *hitquarters.com*: "I was sitting in my office one day when a producer/manager came to see me. He managed the Lewinson Brothers, a team of producers who have since worked with Joss Stone and others.

"He played me their productions and suddenly this voice came on, and I asked, "Who the hell is that?!" and he said, "I can't tell you; it's something that we've done for 19 Management which we have to keep very quiet."

"I said he'd have to tell me what it was, but he wouldn't do that."
Beese continued: "It took me months to find out who it was just by continually asking around. I called 19 Management, but they wouldn't return my telephone calls.

"Finally, I bumped into Felix Howard, who had been writing with the Sugababes, and he played me some songs that he'd been working on. I recognized the voice and asked him who it was and he said that it was Amy Winehouse.

"All in all, it took me about six months to actually find her."

In the meantime, 19 Management had been busy. Amy had begun recording songs, and had signed a publishing deal with EMI.

Communication between different departments at large companies can sometimes be a problem. So it was that, although EMI had Amy's publishing rights, their record label sat on their thumbs rather than sign her up.

When Beese finally tracked down Amy, he spied his chance. He introduced her to his Island boss, Nick Gatfield, who shared his enthusiasm. While EMI were still thinking about it, and with Virgin also interested, Island/Universal got her to sign a recording contract.

The EMI deal meant Amy had enough money to get a place of her own, and she wasted no time in reconnecting with Juliette Ashby, her oldest friend. Their respective parents had asked their school to separate them at senior school, and they went more than two years without seeing each other. But Juliette was the person Amy most wanted to live with, and the pair were to share an apartment for several years.

It was important to Amy that she did not change now she was on the verge of a showbusiness breakthrough. Juliette helped keep her grounded, and would always continue to treat her just the same however much success she had.

As far as Juliette was concerned, there was no jealousy of her friend. Like Amy, she was a singer/songwriter, but she never got her big break and would continue to work as in telesales while Amy toured the world.

"From day one we've always had the same kind of goals, ambitions," said Juliette.

"I sing, and I write songs as well, and to be able to see her making a success of it brought us closer together. There's no jealousy there. Some of her other friends started acting a bit weird and starstruck. But if I see Amy on TV, I just think, 'Oh, there's Amy the Dickhead again.'"

Through EMI, Amy had already been put in contact with producer Salaam Remi who helped her put together her first demos. That working relationship quickly bore fruit, and by the time Island signed her she had penned five songs which were to end up on her debut album, among them "I Heard Love Is Blind", "In My Bed" and "Take The Box."

Remi had started out as a keyboard player, appearing on the 1986 Kurtis Blow hit "Kingdom Blow". By the end of the 1980s he had begun mixing records, though it took him some time to establish his reputation.

He produced The Fugees' 1996 single "Fu-Gee-La", but it was another seven years before his producing career really took off, when he began working with Nas and Mis-Teeq as well as Amy.

Having had to wait so long before tracking down Amy, let alone signing her, Darcus Beese might have expected the hard work was over.

He would not be the last to find, though, that the singer could be difficult to deal with.

Beese said later: "Amy is a law unto herself. She is very strong-willed and sometimes that's frustrating, but that's how it is when you're dealing with potentially great artists who are very confident in what they're doing."

It was no secret that Amy was a perfectionist by nature. She could see the potential of a project from all angles which is why she had to have her way. The potential she saw was beyond anything material, for she was an artist through and through. She could see the impact a song would have on others, could grasp the impact the delivery of the song would make, and understood what was needed to carry it off.

Nick Godwin had a job not everyone in the music business would have coveted – that of Amy's manager. He admitted: "She can be very frustrating," but added: "I don't have an issue with her frankness. She's a real artist who's going to make records for years to come. Someone passionate who speaks their mind and isn't interested in money."

It proved impossible for Beese to guide Amy in the same way he was doing for the Sugababes, whose career he resurrected in 2001.

Having been dropped by London Records after disappointing sales of their debut album "One Touch", and seen founder member Siobhan Donaghy walk out during a promotional tour of Japan, the Sugababes were in dire straits. Within months, Beese had signed them to Island and helped their first single with the label "Freak Like Me" reach the top of the UK charts.

It was clear to him that promoting Amy would be a very different matter. Unlike the Sugababes, she had no residual fan base and her music, he was the first to admit, was unlike anything else in the charts.

Though he worked very closely with Fuller and 19 Management, Beese felt shows like *Pop Idol* had starved the public of genuine new talent. The TV talent shows had produced artists, he believed, who were "about penetrating the Top 5 as many times as possible with singles and then selling albums off that."

In contrast, he was convinced that Amy's success would come off the back of albums.

For her own part, while Amy was as critical as Darcus about the *Pop Idol* phenomenon, she did acknowledge there had been one upside to its success. The TV talent show had introduced a jazz section into the competition, and it had made the link in viewers' minds between the old jazz standards and young artists, so she felt people were more amenable to "buying into an older sound" at the time she was coming onto the scene.

Beese's concept for marketing Amy was for it to be "very organic", and build from a small base. Her debut gig sold out a 1,500-capacity venue, and he said: "those first 1,500 were the most important people of the campaign, because that's what we were going to build upon." He added: "We knew that if we could reach the first 20,000 buyers, they would be real Amy fans and they would establish her fan base."

The other key difference Beese found with Amy, compared to the likes of the Sugababes, was that BBC Radio 1, the traditional home of chart records on the British Broadcasting Corporation, were simply not interested in her.

He was smart enough to realize, though, that radio audiences had changed over the previous decade and that it was now BBC Radio 2 which commanded the higher listening figures.

Beese said: "Radio 2 supported her right from the start. That helped us to get the album to where we wanted it to be, because Radio 2 listeners are generally album buyers."

The label knew that, if they played it right, they had a potential star on their hands because she had the kind of fresh, outspoken attitude the press would lap up. The Jewish girl from North London, who sounded like a black girl from the American Deep South, was about to become a media darling.

"FRANK"

It was a good thing the team behind Amy Winehouse had decided to concentrate on album sales.

Her debut single, "Stronger Than Me", entered the charts on October 6, 2003 and got no higher than 71 in the UK chart. It was hardly encouraging.

Though it was to go on and win the Ivor Novello Award for Best Contemporary Song Musically & Lyrically the following year, it was to be the worst performing single of her career.

Still, the album launch was only three weeks away and her management were confident it would be a success.

It was not a confidence she completely shared. She would later say she was "only 80 per cent behind the album", as she was unhappy that Island had included certain songs and mixes she disliked. A year after its release, she told the media she had "never heard the album from start to finish."

Many people, breaking into the music business, would be content to hand over much of the decision-making to others. And having never produced a record, Island might have expected Amy to simply follow direction. If so, they were to be disappointed.

"I know what I want to do before the other person is even in the room," she said, explaining why she was not good at working with others.

"Making the album I was very focused. Maybe in years to come I will be a good collaborator but at that point I was, like, Look, here is my music. We need brass on this, or that needs to be faster. And I don't want strings. If you want to work with me and you love strings, then go home.

"I probably earned a reputation as a difficult person, because I wrote my own songs and I didn't need people in the studio with me. Not to be rude, but these people would be trying to write pop songs! And I would say, Who are you writing for? What session are you on? Get out. But then I'd waste a day trying to be nice to the person. I'd waste studio time letting them do what they wanted, because I thought it would be the polite thing to do."

Like many great artists, she realized what her gifts were. She knew how to exploit them through artistic means, and understood that no one else in the world was capable of replicating the art she was creating, which is why others should not be given too much control over her projects.

As well as providing the only vocals on the album, Amy played guitar and piano.

If her family and friends had expected her to make a straightforward jazz album, they were to be surprised. She explained: "I take a lot from jazz musically and a lot from hip-hop lyrically. I am a jazz singer but my album is straight hip-hop... I would say that people in creative hip-hop are the jazz of today." Confusingly, as far as her fans were concerned, she would also later describe the record as "beat-driven jazz."

With a voice which was a glimpse into times past, Amy's desire to mingle the past with modern hip-hop was experimental, daring, and cutting edge. She removed the boundaries created by genres and labels, and created what she wanted on her terms. Her music changed the modern perception of what jazz or hip-hop could be, and is truly post-post-modern.

Whatever it was, it was different. And Amy felt it sent out a message to people of her generation.

She said: "The reason I do that is I want kids to listen to my music and think 'I can write whatever I want to write, I don't have to sound like Dido, I don't have to sound like Robbie Williams, and I certainly don't have to go on *Pop Idol* to be able to write music'. I would like real music to come through, just for people who are growing up now, I would hate for them to think they have to sound like someone else to get somewhere."

Of the 13 tracks, she wrote or co-wrote 11. The only exceptions were cover versions of "Moody's Mood for Love" and "(There Is) No Greater Love".

The album title, "Frank", reflected the at times brutal honesty of Amy's lyrics. Several of the songs were inspired by the still raw emotions she felt over the ending of her first serious relationship. That was with a man called Chris, seven years older than her, who she reportedly met while working at the *News of the World*.

Analytical and precise, she did not refrain from exposing her most intimate thoughts about herself in others through her music. Art would continue to be her means for understanding and dissecting her relationships with others, especially men.

Though she said songs on "Frank" were about her relationships in general – with her dad, her brother, even her canary, it was Chris who was central to the album.

Amy said "Stronger Than Me" was written during one of her several reconciliations with Chris. She said: "I guess what I find interested is the relationship two people can have with each other and how badly that can get messed up sometimes.

"We had already split up a couple of times and I know that when you get back together, all the little things that annoyed you about them are going to annoy you 10 times more, but I didn't understand why we weren't supposed to be together.

"Then it just came to me one day, 'you should be stronger than me, I'm the girl and you're the boy. You're seven years older than me and you should be someone I can come to at the end of the day with my problems, not add to them.' And I guess I wrote 'Stronger Than Me' when I realized he was a big girl."

"Take The Box", she said, was about one of the times they split up, and came to divide their possessions.

"When I say 'Frank's in there and I don't care,' that is literally a Frank Sinatra CD. He bought me it for Christmas and I was putting all his stuff in a box, like his T-shirt that I used to sleep in. He bought me Frank Sinatra's 'In The Wee Small Hours' – ironically, cos it's one of the classic heartbreak albums of all time."

Amy chose the album's title partly in honor of Sinatra, though at other times insisted it was named after her dog.

Remi was only one of the producers to work on the album, with half of the disc being produced by a combination of Commissioner Gordon, Jimmy Hogarth and Matt Rowe.

When talking about the production on the album, Amy was always most effusive in her praise of Remi, who also played bass on the disc.

"While I have written about times in my life that have given me trouble and there are points on the album where I am really upset and really angry, I'll always put a punch-line in there and I'll always make it funny," she said.

"Salaam drew me out of myself musically. Because, while I'm a really wacky songwriter, he's exactly the same. He'll always strive for something really different, and I'd never met anyone who can tap into an artist the way he can. Which to me is the mark of a great producer.

"With Salaam I feel like musically anything can be done - and I've never felt like that when working in England, where they don't wanna listen to a girl who thinks she knows what she's talking about. Basically all they care about in this country is listening to the record company."

The album entered the UK Chart at No. 60, and was a slow climber, peaking No. 13 the following January. The success of her second album re-ignited its sales, "Frank" re-entering the UK charts at No. 22, and it had been certified triple platinum by the time she died. It would not be released in the USA, however, until four years after it first charted in the UK.

"Stronger Than Me" had not been a successful vehicle for promoting the album, despite the release of a video for the song.

As 2004 began, the record company hoped that successive singles from the album would reflect "Frank's" rise up the charts. Sadly, none of the other three singles reached the UK top 50, with "Take The Box" doing best by peaking at No. 57.

The fact that the other two singles were double-A sides – "In My Bed/You Sent Me Flying" and "Fuck Me Pumps/Help Yourself" – yet only reached 60 and 69 respectively seemed to back up Beese's conviction that she was principally an album artist.

Releasing a song with a swear word in the title is rarely a miss with the fans, though no doubt a few were left searching the internet for the definition of "Fuck Me Pumps". Also known as "FMPs", these are the high-heeled, open-backed shoes favored by some women out on the town. Amy sarcastically drew attention to these kind of women on her video.

Most of the songs on the album, though, were about her relationship with men. Not just her ex-boyfriend, but her father.

Nine co-writers, including Amy, were credited with writing the song "What Is It About Men?", but the lyrics were all hers. "It's me trying to work out my dad's problems with sticking with one woman, trying to make sense of why he did certain things," she said.

"I completely understand it now. People like to have sex with people. I don't begrudge my dad just because he has a penis. What's the point?"

Mitch, eager to play down his influence, believed that "only the first part" was about him. He said: "The rest of it is more generally about what rats men are. But the song's given me pause for thought, because the divorce obviously colored her view of men."

Amy described herself as "a man's man", though was quick to stress she wasn't a lesbian. Intelligent and busy with nervous energy, she was the sort of woman whose mind was constantly working. She was an effective communicator as is evidenced by her profesional interviews with the media, and she appreciated the way men communicated with one another.

She explained: "Men are far more straightforward. They don't dwell on things and play psychological games. On the whole men are more easy-going and don't piss time up the wall. Life's short. Anything could happen, and it usually does, so there is no point in sitting around thinking about all the ifs, ands and buts.

"All the songs I write are about human dynamics, whether it's with girlfriends, boyfriends, or family. When I did 'Frank', I was a very defensive, insecure person, so when I sang about men it was all like, 'Fuck you. Who do you think you are?'"

One song that showed the extent of Remi's influence on Amy was "In My Bed", which he wrote and produced for her. The track – the third single from the album, released in April 2004 – used the same beat as rapper Nas' hit of the previous year, "Made You Look". That song in turn contained a sample of the Incredible Bongo Band's 1973 cover of "Apache", with both tracks having been penned and produced by Remi.

Some critics felt the label's tinkering with her songs were a negative. Rolling Stone wrote: "Its highlights are more moments than songs - the Stevie Wonder chords of "You Sent Me Flying," the way Winehouse rides producer Salaam Remi's beat on "In My Bed," the smirking tone of the infidelity confession "I Heard Love Is Blind"."

The UK reaction, though, was almost all positive, helping push the album into the top 20.

The *Guardian* newspaper's Beccy Lindon wrote: "Sitting somewhere between Nina Simone and Erykah Badu, Winehouse's sound is at once innocent and sleazy...There are contradictions - but it's hard not to hear the honesty and soul that resonates throughout this album."

Dan Cairns, in *The Times*, described Amy's voice as "A cracked, racked husk that will one moment coo at the object of her affection, the next emit a caustic rasp at the target of her scorn, it harks back to Billie Holiday in its emotional vulnerability, to Joni Mitchell when it eases through the octaves, and to Macy Gray as it lays bare its owner's feelings.

"(It is) a staggeringly assured, sit-up-and-listen debut, both commercial and eclectic, accessible and uncompromising."

The *BBC's* Greg Boraman wrote: "Winehouse combines a distinctive '20 a day' voice with a serious appreciation of female jazz & soul heroes (Sarah Vaughan's scatting style seeps through Amy's vocal ad-libs as well as getting a name check).

"She combines considerable jazz guitar ability with a classic approach which produces a contemporary, quirky, up front, tongue in cheek and risqué lyrics."

Reviewing "You Sent Me Flying" retrospectively, the influential British music magazine *NME* said: "(It) strips it right down to a simple piano accompaniment to showcase Amy's unrivalled vocal talents before adding a simple breakbeat halfway through.

"His message was brutal but the delivery was kind" she sings halfway through the tale, and you're right there with her throughout."

Though it was not reflected in sales to quite the extent Island would have hoped, "Frank" was a critical success and received a nomination for Mercury Prize in 2004. Amy was nominated for the BRIT Awards in the categories of "British Female Solo Artist" and "British Urban Act".

Though the USA would remain an untapped market for Amy until after the release of her follow-up album, "Back to Black", her debut was a hit across Europe. It reached No. 7 in Austria, went platinum in both Germany and Switzerland and reached No. 11 in France.

To Amy, though, it was something to build on. Asked directly by an interviewer whether she was happy with the album, she said: "Yes and no."

She added: "If I'd been 100 per cent satisfied then I could have relaxed and gone on holiday for six months. But it's a constant thing for me to better myself.

"I've got a clear ambition now, to make a record of what I hear in my head. Like Stevie Wonder did. It was a learning curve. I always thought I would do music, but I certainly didn't expect to have a record deal by the time I was 19."

The best thing about her success, she felt, had been receiving the Ivor Novello accolade. "The Ivor Novellos are a songwriter's awards and that's what I am," she said.

"I'm not trying to be the best female, I'm just trying to write songs."

DEALING WITH FAME

In the summer of 2004, Amy Winehouse was feeling disillusioned.

She had wanted her big break, and got it before she turned 20. But "Frank" was not the album she had set out to make.

"The marketing was fucked, the promotion was terrible. Everything was a shambles," she said. "It's frustrating, because you work with so many idiots...they know that they're idiots.

"I hate them fuckers, man. I've not seen anyone from the record company since the album came out and I know why ... 'cos they're scared of me. They know I have no respect for them whatsoever.

"Look ... I know its a terrible thing for someone to come out and say they hate their own music. It's the worst thing you can do. My album isn't shit. If I heard someone else singing like me I would buy it in a heartbeat."

That summer, she eased her frustrations by playing some major gigs. She appeared at Glastonbury, the largest annual summer festival in the UK, the V Festival and the Montreal International Jazz Festival.

The fans wanted to hear all the tracks from "Frank", but though she obliged her mind was beginning to turn away from the jazz influences of that debut and towards the girl groups of the 1950s and 1960s.

While doing promotion for her first album, she was continually having ideas for songs for a follow-up. She interrupted one interview, with Paul Du Noyer from *The Word* magazine, the write down a lyric she had just thought of on a scrap of paper produced from her bag.

Writing "Frank" hadn't been hard, she said, "it's doing all this promo shit that is the really hard work. The only thing you have to remember when writing is, Be honest, always. But with promo it's always, Shut your mouth, Amy! Smile!"

It did not sit easily with such a self-confident young woman. She said she had decided to let the label direct the promotional push, because she had no experience, but it soon became obvious she had little respect for those in charge.

She called her decision to cede promotional control to the label "the wrongest thing I could have done."

"All they know how to do is what's already been done and I don't want to do anything that's already been done," she told Henrietta Rousoullis of the *Independent* newspaper in the UK.

"I don't ever want to do anything mediocre. I hear the music in the charts and I don't mean to be rude, but those people have no soul.

"Learning from music is like eating a meal - you have to pace yourself. You can't take everything from it all at once. I want to be different, definitely. I'm not a one trick pony. I'm at least a five-trick pony."

She was a visionary. She was not willing to risk her artistic integrity in order to follow their formula for success in order to earn money. Amy knew her visions would not only result in great art, but were ideas which had come before their time, and would pay off in a material way.

Roussoullis asked her whether she might become a diva. "I'm probably already one," said Amy, "if that means that you don't give a shit about people's opinions.

"I don't suffer fools gladly. I'm not here to make friends. I've learnt that the hard way - I used to not say things like "I really want to hold a guitar in my video", because I was trying to make everyone like me. But I don't give a shit now."

She enjoyed UK tour she undertook to promote "Frank". It was her first, and she could identify with the audience as it had been just months since she was attending gigs herself.

Playing at the Academy in Brixton, South London, brought back memories of her first visit to the venue, aged 17, when she saw Erykah Badu.

"She was amazing," Amy recalled. "A real drama queen who had the whole crowd in the palm of her hand. I was so blown away that, about 45 minutes into the set, I passed out. I remember feeling the blood drain from my face.

The next thing I knew, I was on the floor with about 10 people staring down at me, and my A&R man's finger shoved into my mouth to stop me biting my tongue. Then the bouncer came and hauled me off to the medical unit, where I spent the second half of the set with my legs in the air."

Island's latest star found that her fame soon spread. Despite being half-American, and sounding Afro-Caribbean, she remained almost unknown in North America but her albums were selling well beyond Europe.

On the continent, "Frank's" highest chart position was No. 6, in Spain, and it made the top 40 in Belgium, Denmark, Greece, Ireland, Italy, Poland and Portugal as well as reaching No. 25 in New Zealand.

After her tour ended, she was able to take time off but a notepad was never far from her side as she sought inspiration for tracks for her second album.

In late 2004, Amy contributed a song, the Carole King ballad "Will You Still Love Me Tomorrow?" to the soundtrack for the film "Bridget Jones: The Edge of Reason".

Nearly three years were to pass, though, from the release of her debut album before she had anything else ready for public consumption.

BETWEEN ALBUMS

Amy Winehouse was far from being the first singer/songwriter to draw inspiration from the pain of lost love.

Joni Mitchell, one of the most successful album-driven female artists of all time, has had most of her success singing about sorrow and break-ups.

American bluegrass star Alison Krauss might not write her own songs, but she has won more Grammys than any other singer with whole albums full of sad songs.

She says: "There's something so raw going on. It's real. Through all this stuff and music and those sad places, you may get so sad but you also experience incredible joy at the same time."

One of Krauss' stand-out songs, her 2003 collaboration with Brad Paisley, is "Whiskey Lullaby." In the light of what happened on July 23, the chorus seems almost to have been written about Amy, or at least a male version of her. It talks about a man "putting a bottle to his head" and "pulling the trigger."

When Amy came to write her second album, it was alcohol and lost love that were most on her mind. Her music was one of the only outlets which allowed her to mourn the loss of her lovers, as is evidenced during songs like "Rehab" and "Back To Black" where deeply painful words were sung amidst catchy choruses as if she wished to share her grief - but only enough to let listeners know what the song was truly about - hidden within another song telling another story. She told several stories in each song, one of which was the truth, and invited listeners to decide which story was the true to them.

Life on the road is one hotel after another, each with a late-opening bar, and a party every night after the gig.

Amy was only 20 when "Frank" was released, but had already been living apart from her parents for two years.

Money was not a problem, there were always friends and other musicians to hang out with, and drugs and alcohol were freely available.

When she turned 20, she told the press she was aware she was smoking too much cannabis, and said her breakfast consisted of Jack Daniel's and Coke.

John Pareles wrote, in the *New York Times* in 2008: "Addiction might start with experiments by performers so young they feel invulnerable…rock stars weren't the first musicians to drink or drug themselves to death.

"What's different, in the 21st century, is that we can watch the breakdowns almost as they happen. In the '60s and '70s there were occasional photos of Janis Joplin hoisting a bottle of Southern Comfort, and word-of-mouth about many bands' backstage excesses or drunken exploits, but those were occasional glimpses and dispatches. Rockers dosed themselves, mostly, behind closed doors."

Amy's management and record label realized she could be a huge star. They also knew that any attempts to make her do something, or not do something, against her will would be in vain.

She had shown as a teenager, before her first record was released, that she was headstrong. Now she knew she was hot property, things would either be done her way or not at all.

If Simon Fuller or Darcus Beese had had their way, Amy's second album would have been an early release to capitalise on the success of "Frank".

Fuller's most famous protégés, the Spice Girls, had released their second album one year after their debut. Beese oversaw the release of the Sugababes' "Three" just 15 months after "Angels With Dirty Faces."

Amy was sick of being asked when her second album would be released, while publicly putting a positive spin on her hiatus.

Asked by DJ Mark Goodier in the lead-up to the release of "Back To Black" why it hadn't happened sooner, she said: "I wasn't rushed into making a second record, which a lot of artists are, I was very lucky to be afforded the time to be honest.

"After a while they were like 'Do you even want to do another record?' They were lovely to me."

Without doubt, though, Island were hugely frustrated. 2004 had started with "Frank" riding high at No. 17 in the UK album charts, but Amy's tour had failed to keep sales high. By the end of the year, the album was at No. 103.

It was not that Amy had no ambition. Simply that she had fallen in love.

Like many singer/songwriters, Amy's problem when coming to write her second album was that she had poured her heart and soul into the first. Since then, she felt all she had been doing was touring, and there had not been any new romantic relationships worth writing about.

She said: "I was doing gigs for a year and a half after I finished my first album. And then… I didn't have anything to write about… no-one wants to hear a second album about promoting the first one."

In between her touring schedule, she had spent much of her free time drinking and playing pool in pubs near the North London flat she had moved into with Juliette. By her own admission, she was drinking heavily and smoking cannabis.

In one pub, she met a man with a name like a court attorney, but who described himself as a music video assistant.

Blake Fielder-Civil had quit school in his native Lincolnshire and moved some 200 miles to London aged 16. He was in a relationship when the pair met, but they began an affair.

The pair fell deeply in love very quickly – he had her name tattooed behind his ear, she had his inked over her heart. Reportedly, they also inflicted matching scars on each other's arms.

Physically, Blake was absolutely Amy's type. She said: "If I'm checking out a man I'll usually go for someone who is at least five nine, with dark hair, dark eyes and loads of tattoos.

"I just like a man who I can muck about with, and who can take a joke. I admire men who don't take anything seriously, like Dean Martin, who had this amazing ability to distance people from himself. He never talked about troubles with his marriage and would have a line for everything.

"Also Sammy Davis Jr, who treated all that racism like water off a duck's back. He was like, 'Fuck it, I've got music.' That's how I feel."

Amy admitted she felt under an internal pressure to produce her best songs yet. "It's easy to write a million things a day, but it's hard to write something you can really fell proud of," she said.

After meeting Blake, she was first too full of romantic love to give songwriting her full attention, then too drunk and stoned.

Just as with Chris, her relationship with Blake was stormy and it would have surprised few of her friends when, after several months together, the pair split.

Suddenly, the songs started flowing from her pen.

She said: "I didn't have anything to write about 'cos I was doing gigs all the time. After a year and a half I think I fell in love and got my heart broken… and then wrote about it."

Amy had had a "half pleased" reaction to "Frank" – mainly, it was the half of the album produced by Remi.

The idea of Remi sharing production with someone else, though, appealed to her and things fell into place when she met Mark Ronson.

Amy and Mark have a number of things in common. Though he was born eight years before her, he was the child of a London Jewish family and heavily influenced by music from a young age. His father had been a band manager and his stepfather was Foreigner guitarist Mick Jones.

Mark shared Amy's love of hip-hop, becoming a well-known DJ on the New York club scene before he turned 19. He was signed to a recording contract by Elektra and, like Amy, made his breakthrough album in 2003.

"Here Comes The Fuzz" was critically acclaimed and featured the likes of Mos Def, who was one of Amy's favoriteartists. Though it would eventually prove a financial success, early sales were disappointing and Elektra dropped him after just two weeks.

The following year, he formed his own label, Allido Records, a subsidiary of Sony BMG's J Records, and turned his attentions back to producing, which he had first done for Nikka Costa before he signed his Elektra deal.

When Amy and Mark met, they got on straight away. Both had enjoyed a similar amount of success, so there was plenty of mutual respect.

Amy said: "When I went to work with him he just really inspired me and I wanted to impress him, and he was literally the same with me."

On Mark's recommendation, Amy reached out to her mother's native New York to hire singer Sharon Jones' long-time band, the Dap-Kings, to work on the new album.

Ronson later said he enjoyed working with Amy because she was not afraid to say when she didn't like his work.

He signed up for the album, Remi stayed on board and the pair decided to split the production credits between them.

In the summer of 2006, Amy headed back to the studio in the USA ready to make an album she felt would be exactly what she envisaged.

"BACK TO BLACK"

With Amy no longer around to ask, we can only now speculate: was "Back To Black" the album she felt she could never better?

The fact is, it was almost five years from the time the album was recorded to when Amy died. For much of that time, she was a tortured soul, so that goes some way to explaining why she never recorded another album.

In the 57 months between the release of "Back To Black" and her passing, though, she was involved in just two completely new musical releases.

She featured on ex-Sugababes singer Mutya Buena's track "B Boy Baby" from the album Real Girl in 2007, and sang with Mark on a cover of Lesley Gore's "It's My Party" for the Quincy Jones tribute album "Q Soul Bossa Nostra" in 2010.

Certainly, "Back To Black" is the album she will be best remembered for and many regard it as fulfilling the potential she had shown with "Frank."

Having had to keep her fans waiting for three long years for new material, Island needed to deliver with the first single from the album.

Looking back at it now, it's clear that "Rehab" will always be the track Amy is most remembered for.

Released on October 23, 2006, a week ahead of the album, it is her only single to make the UK Top 10. Even before the release of the physical single, download sales had seen "Rehab" enter the charts at No. 19. The following week, it climbed to No. 7, making it Amy's highest charting single by more than 50 places.

The single, written by Amy and produced by Mark, was written about her refusal to enter an alcohol rehabilitation centre after her management encouraged her to go. Though, some would say the song was really about the one verse in which Amy speaks of losing her "baby."

She told *The Sun* newspaper: "Rehab is like Butlins - it's a holiday camp. It's an everyday thing for some people, like going to Tesco's.

"I was having a particularly nasty time with things and just drinking and drinking. My management decided to stop buying for me and said they were taking me to rehab.

"I asked my dad if he thought I needed to go. He said: 'No but I should give it a try.' So I did, for just 15 minutes. I don't need help because if I can't help myself I can't be helped."

It was a winner with the critics. The *NME* called it "fun, fun, fun; a sassy rump-shake that takes a refreshingly DIY attitude towards drug rehabilitation ... trend-setting, edgy pop music."

Joe Queenan, in the *Guardian*, echoed the NME's opinion that the music was not totally original but said it amalgamated "the bouncy, life-affirming, harmless girl-group sound of the Sixties with dark, cheeky lyrics that are more appropriate to the 21st century.

"The music of the Sixties was fine, Winehouse seems to be saying, but the lyrics were inane and the age of innocence is over."

Importantly, the US critics were just as fulsome in their praise. *Rolling Stone* said it was a "must hear song", Billboard said the song was "a better buzz than a double-gin martini", and *Time* said it was "impossible not to be seduced by her originality."

Island, who had released "You Know I'm No Good" in the States, saw "Rehab" climb above it to No.90 despite not being officially released.

After Amy performed the track on the MTV Movie Awards in June, it jumped 38 places to No.10 in the Hot 100, eventually peaking one place higher and being gold-certified.

Despite being released more than two months before the end of 2006, "Rehab" sold well throughout the next year. It was the UK's best-selling record of 2007, made No.1 in Norway and Hungary and reached the top 20 in seven other European countries.

Rolling Stone ranked the single at No. 7 on it's list of the 100 Best Songs of 2007, as well as making it No. 194 on its updated list of The 500 Greatest Songs of All Time. It was named *Time's* best song of the year for both 2006 and 2007.

The song won the Ivor Novello Award for Best Contemporary Song in May 2007, and the following February won Grammys for Record of the Year, Song of the Year and Best Female Pop Vocal Performance.

"Rehab" spawned two official remixes, first by Jay-Z, then by fellow rapper Pharoahe Monch.

Like its lead single, "Back To Black" would prove to be an enduring success. Released on October 30, 2006, it went on to be the best selling album of 2007, being certified five-time platinum by the end of that year. It stayed in the top 10 of the UK album charts for 27 consecutive weeks.

This time, there were no cover songs on the 11-track album. Amy wrote seven of the songs alone, the other four with co-writers. The title track was co-written with Mark, who produced it and five others.

He told *Rolling Stone* that when Amy came to his studio with her ideas, she played him "stuff like the Shirelles and the Shangri-Las and the Angels."

He added: "I got inspired by what she was talking about, and that night I did the drum beat and piano part for 'Back to Black' and put tons of reverb on the tambourine.

"She's deceivingly nonchalant, and when I played it for her the next day, she said, 'It's wicked,' but I couldn't tell if she meant it. Then she was like, 'This is what I want my album to sound like.'

"She would come in every day and play me songs on the acoustic guitar, and we'd try different arrangements to find something that felt authentic. The reason everyone goes back to those Motown records is that there were amazing musicians playing together in a room, and that's what we tried to do."

"Back to Black" was nominated for six Grammys and won five, a feat that put her second on the all-time list for female wins in a single year along with Lauryn Hill, Alicia Keys, Beyonce Knowles, Norah Jones and Alison Krauss. Amy won three of the "Big Four": Best New Artist, Record of the Year and Song of the Year.

Once again, she told journalists, the inspiration for the album had been lost love. But there was a key difference.

"The last album was like "screw you, it didn't work out, it's your fault". This time it's more like very sad and resigned and futile. The album's about giving yourself to someone wholly rather than you being two separate entities."

It was a work that matched her expectations far more than "Frank", she was later to tell a *Telegraph* reporter. "I'm my own worst critic," she said. "And if I don't pull off what I think I wanted to do in my head, then I won't be a happy girl."

The album was a huge success in the UK. Though it was only available for three of the first 10 years of the new century, it was the third biggest seller of the 2000s. Amy won the BRIT Award as Best British Female Artist, and would win a third Novello Award for "Love Is a Losing Game."

"Back To Black" was the UK's best-selling album of 2007, with 1.85 million copies sold over the year.

The second single, "You Know I'm No Good", was released in January 2007 with a remix featuring rap vocals by Ghostface Killah and went on to peak at No. 18 while the title track got to No. 25 in the UK and topped the charts in Greece.

The deluxe edition of the album featured a Live Lounge version the song "Valerie". Written by Mark for his solo album Version, with Amy on vocals, it went on to peak at No.2 in the UK singles chart. The collaboration between the two Londoners had clearly paid off, as Mark won the Grammy Award for Producer of the Year for the album.

Including the deluxe edition, "Back To Black" had sold more than three million copies in the UK alone, even before Amy's death.

As often happens, sales of the album in the USA were reignited following success at the Grammys, and it shot up 22 places to reach a new peak of No. 2 the week after the awards.

A good measure of an album's success is its Metacritic rating, which takes into account a record's general acclaim. "Back To Black" was rated 81 out of 100, indicating "universal acclaim."

New Statesman writer Jude Rogers called it "an astonishing soul record, soaking up the sounds of Motown and 1960s girl groups and spitting them back with panache, glamor and a contemporary twist." In the *Daily Telegraph*, Helen Brown called its music "wall-of-sound bombast with brazenly catchy hooks and smart, modern, soul-scouring lyrics", while *The Guardian's* Dorian Lynskey called it a "21st-century soul classic." The *NME* was one of the few dissenters, reviewer Gavin Haynes giving it a 5/10 rating.

On the other side of the Atlantic, the *New York Times* called the album "a wonderfully time-twisted batch of songs", while the *New Yorker's* Sasha Frere-Jones praised Winehouse's "mush-mouthed approach" and "range and delivery."

Amy reminded people of why singers like Ella Fitzgerald and Billie Holiday had such an influence over large masses of music lovers with their instrumental voices.

But to those listening at the time Back To Black was released, it was clear Amy was an artist who was on the same level as Fitzgerald and Holiday. It was like having a jazz singer from the past resurrected, which was why a buzz surrounded her musical accomplishments.

Having discovered a singer who not only sounded American but was so heavily influenced by American hip-hop and soul, the States fell in love with her. Her US label, Universal, released "Frank" to cash in on her popularity, and her fame spread across the country.

In a poll of United States residents conducted for VisitBritain by Harris Interactive that was released in March 2009, one fifth of those polled indicated they had listened to Amy's music during the previous year.

Praise from within the industry came from, among others, George Michael and Prince. The former Wham! frontman chose "Love Is a Losing Game" as one of his Desert Island Discs, while Prince covered the song on tour.

Amy played a number of US dates, and appeared on shows including *Letterman*, to promote the album in America.

Entertainment Weekly writer Chris Willman was bowled over by seeing her perform an acoustic set in Los Angeles, saying: "It was as if all the emotions in the universe suddenly were coming out of her mouth.

"It was almost like this enormous depth of feeling had nothing to do with her, the tiny figure in ballet slippers and a wife-beater shirt, but that she was somehow channelling it."

She was her usual unflinchingly honest self when being interviewed about the background to the album.

Amy said: "I was drinking a lot ... I was just doing one destructive thing after the other. So, yeah, I was in trouble, I was being quite self-destructive."

She realized she was ill, and went to stay with Mitch for a couple of weeks. Her management came to his house and suggested she enter rehab and she agreed – she said she wanted to avoid an argument.

When she arrived at the clinic, she recalled, she was asked why she was there.

"I was like 'dunno', he goes 'why do you think you're here' and I said 'well I'm in love – I drink a lot but I'm in love do you know what I mean?'

"I said I've just come out of a relationship and I've messed it up and he doesn't know how bad it is yet, and when he finds out what I've done ... he said well you're not an alcoholic, you're a depressive.

"I was like with one eye on the door... I was like 'are we done?' He was like OK, well you should fill out this form. We usually get people to fill out a form. I was like 'well how long is that going to take.

"He was like 'well it will probably be about half an hour. I was like no, no I'm going. I was like 'thank you, nice to meet you. Thank you for your time. I left.

"I was in there for ten minutes. It was funny though… didn't bother me. I got a good song out of it, so it was cool. I believe everything happens for a reason."

She later told journalists she had written "Rehab" by accident while hanging out with Mark.

She said: "We were walking down the street, on our way out to the pool hall, and I sang out of nowhere, like a joke," she said. "And Mark was like, 'Who's that?' I said, 'It's no one, I just made it up.' He's like, you should do that as a song, it's funny. And I was like, it's true."

She claimed to have worked out "Rehab" in just 10 minutes, based on the experience. No doubt executives at Island raised their eyebrows at that comment, bearing in mind how long it had taken her to write the other 10 tracks.

This time, unlike when she refused to reveal the identity of Chris, the inspiration for "Frank", there was no doubting who was being written about on "Back To Black".

Amy said of her time with Blake – which she then believed was in the past – "I suppose the relationship I was in the time was just … we loved each other very much but … at the time it was just not the time for us.

"I mean I was very hurt and I needed to make something good out of a bad situation."

Whether she had appreciated it at the time or not, writing such deeply personal lyrics meant she would not be able to just record the tracks and move on. She was forced to bear her soul on stage in front of thousands of people, which she admitted was an emotional experience.

Amy said: "There is a certain part of the set where I sing four or five of the slower songs in a row ... and they are all sad, all ballads and by the end of it I'm half in tears and I'm like ... why did I... (Laughs) do know what I mean?

"By the end of the four or five songs I'm looking at my bass player and I'm like 'we've got to change the set!

"I cry on stage... I don't bawl and roll around on the floor like Patti Labelle crying but... I cry... yeah... personal songs isn't it! To sing it good I've got to think about how it felt at the time, otherwise I'm just on autopilot, I'm just singing."

Though her second album was much more successful than "Frank", Mitch was to say he had enjoyed her debut more as it had been a happier time in her life.

He said: "The songs were great, innocent-ish. 'Back to Black' obviously sold three trillion copies or whatever but, of course, to me, I can't play the album any more because a lot of the songs are about Blake. It reminds me of a really bad time and part of my recovery is to put that aside."

ALEX

In contrast to what happened at her gigs after the released of her second album, when she looked back on the tour to promote "Frank", Amy would remember it largely with affection.

Touring was still new, she enjoyed seeing new places around the world and she was able to maintain a level, if not of sobriety, then of enough control over her drinking and drug use to be able to perform well in her concerts.

Then she met Blake, and arguably entered the happiest period of her life.

Though Blake was in a relationship when they met – and would later return to his former girlfriend, breaking her heart – the couple straight away found a very deep connection.

One of the reasons Amy took so long to write "Back To Black" was simply that she was happy with Blake.

In theory, that love should maybe have inspired her to write, but many songwriters find it much more difficult to write upbeat, positive songs than ones of sorrow and regret.

She explained: "I always want to feel something. Because I know that I can write a song and deliver it to get it out of me if a situation turns bad. I understand myself so much better after I've written a song about something."

While Amy was ambitious, certainly to make a second album that was more completely satisfying to her than "Frank", she was not prepared to put her relationship with Blake on the back-burner to knuckle down and write and record a follow-up.

She was a contradiction. A wild child who loved to party hard and set her own trends. And at the same time, a romantic soul who yearned to settle down, get married and have a family.

She told *Rolling Stone*, albeit in the immediate romantic haze following her wedding:

"I know I'm talented, but I wasn't put here to sing. I was put here to be a wife and a mom and look after my family. I love what I do, but it's not where it begins and ends."

Another interviewer asked her if she had any unfulfilled ambitions. "Nope!" she replied, "If I died tomorrow, I would be a happy girl."

One of the tragedies of Amy's death would be that she would end her days alone in her flat, mourning the end of the last of her relationships, with Reg Traviss. She frequently spoke of wanting to have children, even in the depths of her addiction.

Mitch told reporters at one point: "She was desperate to have children with Blake and she told me they were trying to have a child but they couldn't. Thank God!

"But now her body is in full working order again she'd love to be a mum."

Amy put together "Back To Black" while she was trying to make sense of what had happened with Blake. The couple had rowed, but she felt they were meant to be together and there were always emotional reconciliations.

When he finally went back to his old love, she was somehow able to get her emotions down on paper and turn them into beautiful songs.

While she was still putting the album together, she met Alex Claire. As had been the case with Blake, the pair got together in a pub.

"I made him buy me a tequila because they were refusing to serve me on account of a golf ball sized lump on my head from the previous night," Amy revealed.

It's easy, with hindsight, to say that Alex should have bought her the drink then left.

While they were still together, Amy would release a remarkable album full of emotion about her lost love for Blake.

In every interview, she would be asked about the lyrics, and in every concert she would be forced to relive those emotions. It was hardly a recipe for success for Amy and Alex's relationship.

Alex was a musician, so it would be surprising if Amy didn't play some of the songs for him while she was putting them together. If the lyrics set off warning bells in his brain, it seems he was assured by her that her feelings for Blake were all in the past.

"She'd say they were over for good," Alex would later recall. "The last time we were together she even promised she'd have the famous tattoo of his name on her left breast removed."

Instead, she compromised by having Alex's first initial tattooed on her ring finger.

Although Amy would insist that she and Blake were over for good, it must have upset Alex to hear and see his ex's name all the time.

Amy told *The Sun:* "Back To Black is when you've finished a relationship and you go back to what's comfortable for you. My ex went back to his girlfriend and I went back to drinking and dark times.

"'Tears Dry On Their Own' is a track about the break-up with Blake, my ex. Most of these songs are about him.

"I shouldn't have been in a relationship with him because he was already involved with someone else - a bit too close to home. The song is about when we split up and saying to myself: "Yes, you're sad but you'll get over it." And I did."

She admitted she still talked to Blake, saying "I believe you can be mates with your ex. I'm still really close to him as a friend and nothing more."

Given that we now know she would later dump Alex and marry Blake, it's easy to see the massive understatement in Amy's admission to the newspaper that "Alex, my boyfriend now, doesn't like me seeing him which is understandable, I guess."

Alex, especially as a singer/songwriter himself, must have been flattered by Amy's interest in him. It's also clear the couple had a sexual chemistry.

After she left him, Alex sold his story to the newspapers. They lapped up his revelations that "she loved to be tied up during sex" and got turned on by having sex in public places.

It's hard not to have sympathy, though, for a man who clearly loved Amy. He wrote on his Myspace page that the break-up had left him "skint, heartbroken and homeless - bad luck comes in threes as the old saying goes, but s**t, what's a man to do?"

Things would get worse for him. All the doubts he must have had about Amy's love for him and her feelings for Blake were suddenly confirmed.

One day, soon after being dumped, he walked into his local pub at 3am and there was Amy, drunk and sitting in Blake's lap. "I saw red mist," he wrote. "I was shaking like a leaf."

Barely a month after leaving Alex, Amy got engaged to Blake. "It's like she cut out my heart, bit a chunk out of it, threw it on the floor and stomped on it," he said.

So quickly forgotten by the woman he loved, Alex got his revenge with his kiss 'n' tell story in the media then disappeared from the limelight.

And how did he feel four years later, on Amy's death? Sometimes silence can speak louder than words. On his Twitter page, after British artist Lucian Freud died aged 88 he wrote "Lucian Freud died. Gutted." Two days later, Amy was dead...nothing.

Ironically, Alex had just released his first album having been signed, like Amy, to Island Records. Anyone visiting the Island official website to find details of his record found only a holding page – a large photograph of Amy, uncaptioned, outlined in black.

BACK WITH BLAKE

While she was with Alex, Amy insisted to journalists – and no doubt frequently to him – that her relationship with Blake was over. They were now "just friends".

Even if we accept that, their reunion was dramatic. Within a month of officially getting back together, Blake had proposed. Four weeks later, the couple were married.

They were in Miami, and went to the courthouse to get a marriage license, with the idea of getting married the next day. Once there, they found the office would be closed the following day and decided, since they were already there, they may as well do it there and then. They paid $130 and were married by a Miami clerk, with no witnesses. Their wedding breakfast was a burger and chips.

Blake told *Rolling Stone's* Jenny Eliscu later the same day: "I don't want to say we did it on a whim, because that makes it sound whimsical."

Eliscu, having been granted two days' access to the couple, said she had "no doubt they are deeply and passionately in love with each other." But she could also see signs of what was to come of their relationship.

She wrote: "There's also the clear sense that Winehouse and Blake are a pair of self-destructive souls equally capable of being the best or the worst thing that's ever happened to each other … They are partners in crime who disappear to the bathroom with such regularity that one can't help but speculate about possible drug use."

For her part, Amy said she had stopped smoking cannabis but was now drinking more, adding: "I suppose if you have an addictive personality then you go from one poison to the other."

Though "Back To Black" was released in October 2006, Amy only played a few initial low-key gigs to promote it. There was less pressure this time around, not only because the humorous video to "Rehab" seemed to be on continuous play on most music channels but because the album sold very well right from the start.

She appeared on the popular "*Jools Holland's Annual Hootenanny*" on British TV on New Year's Eve - joining Paul Weller and Holland's Rhythm and Blues Orchestra to sing Marvin Gaye's "I Heart It Through the Grapevine." – but it was not until the following February when she played a first stretch of 14 gigs.

The first signs of trouble appeared in the summer of 2007, when she only just made it to the *MTV Movie Awards*, where she was to be introduced on stage – at his own request – by Bruce Willis.

She had insisted on spending the hours leading up to the show having a good time in Las Vegas. Amy's reputation had gone before her, and MTV bosses realized they wouldn't be able to dissuade her. "We had to let her go, stay in touch and hope for the best," said an executive.

They did not hear from her again until an hour before the show, when she texted to say her plane had touched down in Los Angeles

Amy played at the Glastonbury Festival for the second time, as well as the Lollapalooza festival in Chicago and Baltimore's Virgin Music Festival.

August brought the first sings of her health problems. She cancelled two opening gigs for the Rolling Stones, and her representative Tracey Miller announced she was canceling the rest of that month's dates "in order to address her health issues".

Denying reports she had entered rehab, Miller said she had been treated for "severe exhaustion" at University College London Hospital and later released.

"She has done hundreds of shows and promotional appearances in the last year, often working 16 hour days. It's bound to catch up with anybody," she said.

Miller's continuing insistence that Amy was merely exhausted were undermined by Blake, who told reporters the pair had checked into a "retreat" in Essex, near London. While not addressing the nature of her problems, he said: "It's not as bad as everyone thinks, but she's fine, she's loved and looked after."

As far as her public perception was concerned, this now gave Amy a big problem. Almost uniquely for a recording artist, she was as open and frank in interviews as she was in her lyrics.

Even when it came to admitting her weaknesses, she was rarely less than honest. She admitted to *The Sun that:* "I'll beat up Blake when I'm drunk … if he says one thing I don't like then I'll chin him."

Her fans, and the world in general, may well have believed her at this point if she had denied she had a problem with drink and drugs.

Blake, though, was a different matter. For one thing, he had already broken Amy's heart, so her fans regarded him with suspicion at best.

The fact that in February – while still with Alex - she had seemed happy and healthy, then within a few months of reunited with Blake she was ill enough to be treated in hospital seemed more than a coincidence to many people.

If he had any standing with the general public at all, it disappeared in one sentence. And he could hardly blame anyone but himself.

Interviewed by *People* magazine, his mother Georgette made an impassioned plea for the couple to stop taking drugs.

She told them: "We're riddled with guilt, we question our parenting.

"Everything goes through your head. Do you wait until they die?" Georgette would also tell the *BBC*: "I think they both need to get medical help before one of them, if not both of them, eventually will die."

Addressing his mother's comments, Blake insisted: "I would say there are a few problems there, but certainly not the magnitude that my mum was falsely quoted as saying." Blake was clearly in denial, but if he thought the world would believe him he was sadly mistaken. The *BBC's* "false quotes" were on tape, for one thing.

It was only once the pair were separated that he would admit having "introduced her to heroin, crack cocaine and self-harming." "I feel more than guilty."

His father Giles seemed to put his finger on the problem when he told the *BBC*: "Georgette and I both believe that they are drug addicts, and they don't believe they are.

"I think they believe they are recreational users of drugs, and they are in control, but it seems to Georgette and I that this isn't the case."

Giles, who said he believed the pair used cocaine, crack cocaine and possibly heroin, was concerned that Amy and Blake could both end up dead. He said: "If one dies through substance abuse, the other may commit suicide."

There was only one way Amy could reassure her fans. She recovered enough to appear at the Mercury Awards, where her performance of "Love Is a Losing Game" was described by one music journalist as "amazing". The audience voted with their feet, giving her a standing ovation.

Feeling better, Amy fulfilled several European dates – showing her unwillingness to lie by telling one German reporter who asked whether she was now drug-free: "That's none of your business".

The answer came several days later, when she was arrested by Norwegian authorities for possessing marijuana.

She and Blake were held in the cells overnight. For Amy it might well have been a wake-up call; for Blake it was a small taste of what was to come.

CHRISTMAS ALONE

When people had read Amy's admission that she was prone to "kick the shit" out of Blake, they might have got the impression he was a battered husband.

What was not known at that time, and only came to light much later, was that in June 2006 he had beaten up bar owner James King. The landlord had suffered a fractured cheekbone.

It wasn't even a fair fight – Blake had ganged up with his friend Michael Brown, who had an unspecified grievance against King. At around the time the bar closed, the pair pounced on the landlord, kicking him to the ground and injuring him.

The attack was caught on closed circuit TV, and the two men were later arrested.

Though Blake and Amy were not together at this time, they were in contact and it's highly likely that he told her. What we will never know, though, is whether he ever told her what he would do in late 2007, six months into their marriage.

As often happens, there was a long delay between the arrests and the case being set for court. Some 16 months after the assault, King received a visit from two "heavy-looking men", Anthony Kelly and James Kennedy, who told him he had to withdraw his statement.

King later told the court: "I was I would need to write a withdrawal of my statement which would need to be videoed. I was told that I would have to say that I was under duress — which was as far from the truth as possible.

"Apparently the video was for Amy Winehouse. It seems they were extorting her for money to make this go away." The men returned another day and threatened him again, he said.

At the eventual trial, *Daily Mirror* journalist Stephen Moyes told how he had been contacted by Kelly in October 2007. They had tried to sell the paper the security camera images of the attack, but also boasted that there was an "even bigger story".

Moyes said: "He [Kelly] said that the victim of the assault, James King, was to be taken out of the country and paid some money so that it [the trial] would not happen. He was to be paid £200,000."

Moyes said he had asked Kelly whether Amy knew about the deal and was told "Who do you think is paying for it?"

The following month, King withdrew his statement.

Prosecutor Sean Larkin said there was no evidence Amy had been in on the plot.

However, he told the court: "On November 7, Amy Winehouse's manager asked her bank for £8,000, which was withdrawn on November 8. The manager asked for more cash and Winehouse asked for £5,000, which she collected from the office in person.

"That may well accord with the £5,000 he [Kelly] wanted up front, which he later told Stephen Moyes he had received."

We can only speculate on what, if anything, Amy knew about this whole situation. Clearly, though, Blake was a worried man during this whole time. The initial assault charge might have been enough to put him in jail, away from Amy, and he saw an opportunity to make it go away.

On November 8 2007, the game was up. There was a knock on the door and within a few minutes a handcuffed Blake was being led away from a hysterical Amy by eight policemen.

Now he knew he had been double-crossed by the men he had hired to do his dirty work, and there would be no dodging prison.

Blake and Amy's world came crashing down around them. They had been looking forward to a first Christmas as a married couple; instead Blake charged, denied bail and put in prison on remand.

Within a fortnight, Amy was to start the next leg of her tour, a 17-date stint opening at the National Indoor Arena in Birmingham. Considering what she was dealing with – a husband in prison and a battle with addiction – what followed was hardly surprising.

A full house of 12,700 people were thrilled as she walked on stage, but they were soon booing and many walked out.

A music critic for the *Birmingham Mail* said it was "one of the saddest nights of my life...I saw a supremely talented artist reduced to tears, stumbling around the stage and, unforgivably, swearing at the audience."

Reportedly, she told the audience: "To them people booing, wait 'til my husband gets out of incarceration. And I mean that."

It was to be a similar story elsewhere. The audience at the Hammersmith Apollo were already booing before she took the stage, 45 minutes late.

The *NME* wrote: "Midway through the performance Winehouse seemed bored and walked offstage, leaving a backing singer to step forward and take vocal duties.

"She looked unstable throughout the set and at one point her beehive hair extension nearly fell off.

"While performing 'Valerie' as part of the show's encore, Winehouse left the stage again, halfway through the song, this time for good, once more leaving a backing singer to fill in until the show ended."

Fans posted on forums that she had been "clearly drunk" on stage.

Drunk or not, it was clear Amy understood that illusions could be powerful. Through her fashion sense, words and strategic collaborations with other artists, she showed that she knew how to manipúlate people's perceptions of her by creating an illusion which only she could control. The moment she lost interest in keeping the illusion alive, it crumbled for all too witness. In this respect, she most likely never felt she was a victim of circumstance, but understood she was the decisión-maker, and whatever came of her career would be on her terms.

The next day concert promoters Live Nation announced she was cancelling the rest of the tour. Officially, the reason was "the rigors involved in touring and the intense emotional strain that Amy has been under in recent weeks."

The statement added: "In the interests of her health and wellbeing, Amy has been ordered to take complete rest and deal with her health issues."

Once again, fans' credibility was being stretched by people purporting to speak for her. Once again, Amy came through with the truth. "I can't give it my all onstage without my Blake," she wrote on her website.

"I'm so sorry but I don't want to do the shows half-heartedly; I love singing. My husband is everything to me and without him it's just not the same."

Canceling the tour at least meant Amy could stay close to her husband, jailed in London's Pentonville Prison. But if she took any comfort in that, it was short-lived.

Blake failed a drugs test, reportedly testing positive for heroin. The couple, who had been able to meet in an open hall with officers patrolling, were now reduced to seeing each other through a glass screen, with no physical contact allowed. It was too much for Amy, who stopped visiting.

That was welcome news for her mother, who hoped that being separated from Blake would allow Amy to start putting her life back together. Janis had greeted her son-in-law's incarceration by telling reporters: "Thank God he's gone inside. Everyone else can see it. But Amy chooses not to."

The Fielder-Civils had used the media to try to get through to the couple, and now it was Janis' turn.

She wrote a letter to Amy, through the *News of the World*, telling her: "All you have to do is come to us and we'll do everything in our power to get you well again. After all, you are still my baby and you always will be."

Janis added: "Wherever you are, whatever you need, we're here for you day and night. I hope you know that."

A week before Christmas, Amy was in hell on her own in the house. Her husband in jail, her fans seemingly turning against her, unable to perform, it seemed her life could get no worse.

It could. On December 19, she was arrested in connection with the investigation into perverting the course of justice – the same matters facing her husband.

Though released after giving fingerprints and a saliva swab to police, she spent Christmas wondering whether 2008 would see her facing charges.

FAMILY

When Amy died, it was natural for both Mitch and Janis to ask themselves whether they could have done anything to save her.

Both will have felt a sense of guilt. For Mitch, it was made even worse by the fact that, at the time, he was in the USA trying to launch his own singing career. To some, it made it look like he was trying to exploit his daughter's fame at a time when she needed him the most.

Their history was proof enough that the two shared an intimate bond, not only as father and daughter, but as true friends. From having "Daddy's Girl" tattooed on her arm to unabashed statements about her love for her father, it was evident that Amy felt close to her mother and father, and those feelings were reciprocated. Any insinuation depicting Mitch as a man selling his daughter out for a singing career is unfounded.

That would be unfair on Mitch, who would have done anything for Amy. He admitted to one reporter, "I've said it myself a hundred times, if I wasn't Amy's dad, I wouldn't get to make an album," but said it was she who urged him to record an album.

As far as being absent at the end, in his heart Mitch will have known there was nothing he could have done. She might have had a "Daddy's Girl" tattoo, but Amy was too headstrong to take his advice.

Compared to the Fielder-Civils, Mitch often came across in the media as being the parent who was least concerned.

That was merely a front, for her brother Alex later insisted: "We all knew how bad her condition was. There was never any denial on the part of my parents, whose fears and anxiety over their only daughter had made them both ill. Dad was on the verge of a breakdown."

Mitch had heard Blake's parents being interviewed on a *BBC* Radio talk show, when Giles Fielder-Civil had urged fans to stop buying Amy's records in order to send a message to the singer that she had to stop taking drugs. He called up the show, sympathising with Giles' intentions but saying he was certain a boycott simply wouldn't send any message to his daughter.

"Believe me, my first instinct is to get hold of her, pick her up and take her back to my house and lock her away," he would say later.

"But I've spoken to the finest drug counselors in the world, and they've said that is exactly the wrong thing to do."

One incident, above all, showed Mitch just how powerless he was to change Amy.

Desperate to get her to stop taking heroin, he faked a heart attack. He told the *Mirror*: "I just didn't know which way to turn. I'd tried everything.

"I pretended I was seriously ill and even got our doctor to tell Amy that I was dying.

"Once I even started screaming and said I was having a heart attack, but it didn't work. Amy's not stupid and she wanted to see my medical records proving I was actually ill."

Mitch had no cause to beat himself up over the fact that he had broken up the family home by moving out when Amy was nine.

It happens in millions of homes across the country, for many different reasons, and doesn't always have a negative effect on children. Amy herself admitted she thought Mitch had done the right thing.

As for Janis, she had her own problems. Diagnosed with MS in 2003, she would have sought support from her daughter but over time, Amy grew more distant.

Janis recalled: "To begin with, after she left home, she would ring me every day. I was never frightened of losing her because there was always contact.

"Then, once she started travelling more and working in America, I started to feel a detachment. Looking back, it built up over time."

Perhaps not wanting to add to her mother's troubles, Amy for a long time hid her own issues. As far as Janis was concerned, Amy "always had a very good appetite", and it came as a shock to her when she eventually admitted she had bulimia and anorexia.

When she talked about self-harming, she told Janis it was something one of her friends was doing. "I never realized then she might have been talking about herself," Janis said.

Amy also never spoke to her father about why she cut herself, though Blake told him his rationale. Mitch told *the Times* newspaper: "He explained to me that when they're going into [drug] withdrawal, if they cut themselves, it takes away the pain."

Probably Mitch had long since abandoned the idea he might one day get to walk his daughter down the aisle to her wedding. And indeed, with Blake waiting at the end, one suspects he would have refused to let go of her arm.

In the end, Amy didn't even tell her parents she was getting married until after the fact.

One of her friends, though, had called them both up the day before to warn them – specifically, to warn them that the couple had not signed a pre-nup. Mitch rang his daughter, begging her not to do it, to no avail.

Janis said: "My feeling is, she wasn't aware of getting married. I think they were probably both so out of it that when he said, 'Let's do it', she said, 'OK, then.'"

Amy sent a clear message to her mother when, on the day her first cheque from publishers EMI cleared, she moved out. Alex described her as "stoical" because she rarely showed her emotions, but there was lots of hurt there. It spoke volumes that Janis never played her daughter's music in the house.

She said: "It's hard and it hurts but I know I can't help her right now. She's got to do that for herself and every day I can only hope she's strong enough to do it."

Perhaps it crossed Mitch's mind that, in choosing "bad boys", Amy was compensating for either his absence from the family home while he was on the road or when he had moved out. It's a popular theory as to why some women seek out men who are clearly wrong for them, but who knows?

At any rate, if Mitch had been powerless to stop Amy reuniting with Blake in early 2007, he drew the line when, with her husband on remand, she started spending time with Pete Doherty.

There was almost no-one else on the planet more unlikely to help Amy get off the drugs.

The singer, convicted of possessing crack cocaine, heroin, cannabis and ketamine, was rarely out of the headlines during his relationship with model Kate Moss and he had shown no signs of mending his ways. Not long before Amy took to hanging out with him, photographs had appeared in the newspapers of him allegedly forcing his pet cat to smoke crack.

Interviewed by *Grazia* magazine in the UK, Mitch pulled no punches with his views on Doherty.

"He's a scumbag," he said. "I flipped when I saw him sitting with Amy backstage at her Brixton gig. That night I went crazy. My wife thought I was going to have a heart attack. I was apoplectic."

While those who loved her were kept at arm's length, Amy was keeping company with those who were out to exploit her. One "friend" filmed her smoking what looked to be a crack pipe, and sold the video to *The Sun*.

Urged by the moralising newspaper to take action, police charged her. *The Sun* were later to report that she had escaped court through a "legal loophole". Police pointed out that all they had to go on was the video, and there was no evidence as to what the pipe had contained.

The paper spoke to Dads Against Drugs founder Rob Broomfield, whose reaction was prophetic. He said: "The tragedy is that we're watching this young woman die in front of our eyes and nothing is being done."

Though Amy would always deny she had had an affair with Doherty, the pair were close for several months.

The relationship between the UK's two most high-profile drug-addicted recording artists was, of course, lapped up by the press.

Doherty, though, did Amy no favors by posting videos on YouTube of the pair in a dark room playing with just-born mice, their fingernails encrusted in black resin, using the animals as puppets to beg Blake not to divorce her.

Amy had always made good copy for the newspapers. There was mock-horror in late 2007 when she was pictured outside, barefoot and dressed only in jeans and a bra.

To the paparazzi, though, getting pictures of Amy looking "tired and emotional" was like shooting fish in a barrel.

One freelance photographer said: "She's on loads of crack, but you can see through that. I just want for her to get better.

"I'm hoping someday for that set of pictures of her riding her bike in the park or something healthy."

WITHOUT BLAKE

CLOSE THE GATE

Somehow, with professional help, Amy found the strength to start performing again. On 20 February she sang "Valerie" with Mark, followed by "Love Is a Losing Game" at the BRIT Awards. She urged the crowd to "make noise for my Blake."

She went on to play in several European cities, including Paris and Lisbon, before performing twice in two days in June – at Nelson Mandela's 90th Birthday Party in Hyde Park in London, then at the Glastonbury Festival.

Having famously said "No, no, no" to rehab, Amy was now willing to be helped. She was a resident at The London Clinic for a while, and took temporary leave to perform at the Mandela celebration and Glastonbury.

Encouraged by being able to sing in public twice in 24 hours, she then opted to be treated as an outpatient.

The combination of a heavy smoking habit and her crack cocaine use, though, caused her health problems.

In June, Mitch told reporters she had been diagnosed with small amounts of emphysema. Her lungs were only operating at 70 per cent capacity, and she had an irregular heartbeat.

British Lung Foundation spokesman Keith Prowse said the condition could be managed with treatment, but that "heavy smoking and inhaling other substances like drugs can age the lungs prematurely".

All the same, Amy's consumption of tobacco was fairly low on her family's list of concerns. They had seen her close to death from her drug addiction, and for her brother Alex her relative recovery was something to celebrate.

Visiting her at her flat, with his girlfriend, he saw her just after she'd taken a hit from the crack pipe, and found it "hard to take in that the barely communicative shell in front of us was my own flesh and blood."

The family was unable to visit her while she was in rehab, so the next time they saw her was when she performed – via satellite link, as she had been initially denied a US visa because of her drug conviction – at the Grammys.

"For the first time in God only knows how long, my parents were truly happy, and Amy was too. So of course was I," wrote Alex. "We hugged and kissed, and suddenly the world melted away; we were alone, a loving family that has suffered so much and – we deeply wish – come out the other side."

Amy told her brother she was off drugs, and didn't miss crack. He said there were "very definite signs that Amy – the real Amy – is back among us. The hope, of course, is that this time it's for real."

It was not the first time those who loved her hoped she had conquered her demons; it would not be the last.

Though consoled by the likes of Pete Doherty, Amy was not about to forget her imprisoned husband. At her Grammys acceptance speech, she told the global TV audience "This is to my mum and dad – and for my Blake incarcerated."

She would shock a *Spin* magazine journalist when, during an interview, she carved "I love Blake" on her stomach with a shard of glass.

Drugs are, of course, illegal in prison but that didn't mean Blake couldn't get hold of them.

Amy might have hoped he would join her in trying to get clean, but it was clear he was still using heroin and indeed would be hospitalised later in the year after a suspected overdose.

Rumours had first appeared in January that Blake wanted a divorce. At the time, a source told the media it was something he just said in the heat of the moment during an argument.

Amy's friendship – if indeed that's all it was – with Doherty would have riled Blake, though. Denied the chance to see his wife on their wedding anniversary, because he was not allowed visitors on a Sunday, he would learn the following day that Amy had spent the day watching Pete play soccer.

If he could score heroin in jail without too much trouble, getting his hands on the newspapers was a piece of cake. So he was able to keep tabs on the stories about all her latest alleged flings.

Some of her friends were indiscreet, certainly when money was on offer from the papers.

Among the men she was reported to have had flings with were actress Sadie Frost's on-again, off-again boyfriend Kristian Marr and Alex Haines, who worked as an assistant at her management company.

When *Rolling Stone* journalist Claire Hoffman came to the flat to do an interview, she didn't even need to ask any personal questions before Amy's friend Nicole Remi let the cat out of the bag.

"How did anyone know about you and Alex and Kristian?" Nicole asked Amy, leaving the singer little room for a denial.

When asked outright by one journalist, Amy insisted: "I am not divorcing Blake. We're going to be together for ever. I don't have a new boyfriend."

In court, that might have qualified as "the truth, and nothing but the truth", but whether it was "the whole truth" was a different matter. Particularly from someone who had gone on record as saying: "I believe in casual sex. I know it's sad that I think cheating on people is fine."

Marr, in particular, gifted *The Sun* a story in May when, returning to her flat, he found himself locked out and unable to wake Amy.

He decided to force his way into her garage to bed down but was soon disturbed by police. The photographers, naturally, were there to snap pictures of him being taken away to the police station.

Island, who had been rumoured to be considering dropping Amy for her own good early in 2008, decided instead to hire Haines to look after her.

That backfired badly when he was taped allegedly smoking crack. Having been previously described by Janis as a "lovely boy" and a good influence on her daughter, he was quickly fired.

One source told the press Blake had been incensed at hearing that Amy and Alex were sleeping together, and that it had "caused massive rows" between the couple.

It should have been clear to Alex from the start that a relationship between a star and her hired help would never be a meeting of equals.

When he was eventually dumped and duly took his pieces of silver from the *News of the World* for his story, he tried to talk himself up as having been her "secret" lover – six months after their sister paper *The Sun* first reported it.

He said: "She would go on about Blake and her being together forever straight after we made love. I sat there in disbelief. We had few bust-ups over it."

You don't say…

In a rare moment of insight, said Alex, she "reckoned she would join the 27 club of rock stars who died at that age." He added: She told me, 'I have a feeling I am gonna die young'."

A CHANCE LOST

February 2008 was a good month for Amy. She was out of rehab, a big hit at the Grammys and – after an anxious two months – was told by police that she would not face charges over the allegations that had put Blake in prison.

Trouble, sometimes self-inflicted, was rarely too far away, though.

By the end of April she was back in the headlines for the wrong reasons, alleged to have headbutted a man in the street. When *The Sun* labelled the incident "her most depraved night yet", readers might have reflected that it was up against some pretty stiff competition.

Amy agreed to visit the police station, turning up at 5pm on Friday. But when a doctor, called by officers, determined she was "in no fit state" to be interviewed, she was locked in a cell overnight and given a caution.

Having tried everything else, Mitch told the *News of the World* it was time for desperate measures. He admitted her rehab had not worked, because she had "not wanted to get clean."

He called for her to be locked up in a mental hospital, for her own protection.

"I want her sectioned," he said. "The situation is getting out of control. I want her off the street."

She was in court to support Blake when pre-trial arguments began in June, the pair blowing each other kisses across the courtroom.

But at some point, he will have told her that he was changing his plea to guilty. Potentially, he was looking at a lengthy jail sentence.

A family friend insisted to *People* magazine that Blake spending an extended period inside "isn't Amy's biggest problem." It was as far as Amy was concerned. She and Blake's parents pinned their hopes on his solicitor convincing the judge that, rather then keeping him in prison, the best option all round would be to release him into rehab.

On the day of the trial, Amy couldn't face going to court. When the judge read out his sentence, hugged co-defendant Michael Brown and his mother let out a gasp of joy. They were mistaken; they thought he was being released to a private drug treatment programme.

Instead, Judge David Radford handed him a 26-month sentence.

"You behaved in a gratuitous, cowardly and disgraceful way," the judge told him. Even allowing for the time he had already served on remand, Blake was told he would not be released until December.

In mitigation, Blake's lawyer told the court his client wanted to stay off drugs and "be a role model for Miss Winehouse."

He added: "It is their intention to divorce themselves from hard drugs and not separate from each other."

Clearly, though, another six months apart was going to place huge strain on the relationship.

They had now been married for more than a year, but Blake had been locked up for more than half that time.

With Blake's role as an enabler for Amy's habit diminished, the Winehouses and Amy's friends had hoped that she could get clean. But it seemed that every time there was a real window of opportunity for Amy to recover, she would slam it shut.

Newspapers reported, in the lead-up to Blake's sentencing, that she had been accused of attacking people four times in the space of a fortnight.

The alleged third victim told the *Mirror* "She suddenly turned and walloped me three times across the face. I hadn't said a word to her or touched her."

Somebody else who, these days, hardly said a word to Amy was her mother-in-law. They seemed close up until the trial, but afterwards Georgette began to blame her for the length of Blake's sentence.

She said: "I feel all the media attention on Amy has probably had an impact on my son's release. That's probably the hardest part of all.

"As a mother, what would any mother think when she sees Amy? It has had a huge impact."

That, at least, was her version. *The Sun* had earlier reported that Blake, offered the chance for a September release providing he live with Georgette in Nottinghamshire, had opted to stay in jail.

Mitch had been trying to put on a brave face, insisting that his daughter would stand by Blake however long he was imprisoned and still talking about her wanting children.

The fear that if she did, the baby would become addicted was motivating her to quit, he suggested.

In the end, Blake was let out in November and, under the conditions of his release, went straight into rehab.

He found, as Amy had earlier in the year, that he was not allowed visitors. Now forced to be apart from his wife, he told the *News of the World* he had decided that a permanent separation was the only way to help Amy.

"I have to let her go to save her life," he said. "I am not abandoning her. I am doing this out of love."

The tragic soap opera of their relationship would run for a few more episodes, however. A day later he escaped from rehab and turned up at the hospital where Amy was being treated.

A witness told *The Sun*: "All hell broke loose - everyone was totally shocked. He was asking Amy to forgive him."

Afterwards, he handed himself over to the police, knowing it would mean a return to prison.

Within a few days came another kick in the teeth. Alex Haines' story appeared in the papers, revealing he and Amy were having sex "four or five times a day", throughout the summer.

Incensed, Blake vented his feelings in phone calls from prison to his wife on her mobile. After a while all he got was her voicemail.

From his cell, he instructed his representatives to file for divorce, citing Amy's adultery.

Mitch later said that Blake had been "winding her up" and "making her life hell" with the calls, and the only way he could intervene was by taking the batteries out of his daughter's phone.

Mitch heard about the divorce petition before his daughter, he told *Hello!:* "I had to call Amy before she heard about it from someone else.

"She asked me, 'Daddy, why does he want to divorce me?' I said, 'You know I don't like him, but I have to admit that your behaviour with another man is not what marriage is all about.'"

The couple had admitted to abusing each other physically. When denied physical contact they would do it verbally. With even that now impossible, the relationship began to be played out via the media – always grateful to have a role.

Amy flew to the island of St Lucia, where she was visited by a *Sun* reporter. "I still love my Blake," she insisted. "I won't let him divorce me. He's still in jail but the moment he comes out I'll be there waiting for him. We're perfect for each other."

It was a velvet glove that contained an iron fist. She admitted she was having a fling with rugby player Josh Bowman on St Lucia, saying: "While Blake is in jail I'm still gonna have a good time - he can't do much about it."

Deserved or not, it was a low blow that Blake - 4,000 miles away from his wife's tropical island hideaway and facing an indeterminate stretch - will have felt right to the bones.

The real knockout blow to their relationship, though, came several days later when Amy spoke to the *News of the World*.

Rather than it being a holiday fling, she was in love with Josh, she told the paper. "For the time being I've just forgotten I'm even married.

"I've finally escaped from hell," she added. "I'll deal with Blake when I get back. But our whole marriage was based on doing drugs."

AMY AFTER DRUGS

Back home, her fans greeted Amy's vow that she was off drugs for good with cautious optimism. If she were now really able to move on with her life, perhaps there would be some new material on the horizon.

It seemed there would. *People* magazine reported that she had returned to the studio to start work on her third album with Mark Ronson.

The pair recorded a song called 'Mission Of Solace' they hoped would be the title track for Daniel Craig's outing as 007 in 'A Quantum Of Solace'.

She said: "I'm excited to be back at work in the studio, enjoying songwriting and making music again."

Mark said that when the pair hung out Amy had played him some new songs. He added: "She doesn't want to make the same record, and I wouldn't want to revisit Black To Black. It cheapens the original."

All seemed well between them, as he described her as "a warm person with a sharp sense of humour and a painfully nonchalant *Sudafed* demeanour."

These polite, optimistic quotes masked the truth, which Amy later confessed to *Rolling Stone.*

"We are close enough that I thought we could be like, 'Hello, darling, it's me,'" she told the magazine, adding that they simply didn't connect.

"I played him tracks I liked, just getting the vibe, and he was like, Amy, come, let's work.' He was really just uptight...." she trails off and then resumes cheerfully: "He left after three days, and I was like, 'Breathe a sigh of relief, I'm in the country and I can write.'"

Though Mark suggested there would be a different feel to the third album, Amy had other ideas.

She told reporters: "I'm gonna do another couple of albums that I've written all myself... cut a few EPs. I've got loads of stuff left over from the last album … not stuff that's written or that's been produced."

It was clear that she had abandoned the early jazz-influenced hip-hop of "Frank". Though it had launched her career, for which she was grateful, she was never really proud of it.

She admitted: "Even when I was at record signings and the store would be playing Frank in the background, I'd be begging them to play something else!"

The style she found for "Back to Black", though, was something she felt she could stick with. She said: "I've got to a point where I've made an album which I'm proud of."

Amy added: "I think I'll probably do the same thing that I've done on this album, just 'cos when I say I've got so many songs left over, it's all of the same ilk – plus it's all I listen to… a lot of sixties stuff.

"I can't really imagine me writing anything that's too far from that… like I've done with 'Back To Black', so it's all I've really listen to is sixties stuff… it's not a conscious decision it just what comes out you know… I'm influenced by what I listen to."

When *Rolling Stone* asked her what her third album would be like, she told them: "Same stuff as my last album but with some ska. When the songs are done, they'll be all atmospheric and cool.

"They might be like these girls I've been listening to, like the Shangri-Las."

Georgette was to later release, to the media, handwritten letters from Amy to Blake in which she told him she would write future albums for him.

A third album, of course, was never made.

When Amy sent her record company the demos she had made in St Lucia they were not impressed, telling her the material was not good enough to be released.

At various times there were reports that Amy was close to finishing the record, with Remi acting as producer.

He was to tell a radio station after she died: "We were working on it; it's not a complete album."

The projected release date kept getting pushed further ahead, and there were never even any demos available on her website.

That was especially frustrating for fans, given that Darcus Beese was quoted as saying: "I've heard a couple of song demos that have absolutely floored me."

Amy's representative told the media that she had recording facilities in St Lucia, and was working on new material out there with Remi.

Amy and Mark were to settle their differences enough to work on "It's My Party" for the Quincy Jones tribute album.

There was also talk of Amy forming a group, that was to feature drummer ?uestlove of the Roots on drums.

Having kicked drugs, for good, in late 2008, maybe Amy was able to see past her own problems for the first time in a long while.

She had always been close to her goddaughter, Dionne Bromfield, and early in 2009 she decided to help launch 13-year-old Dionne's musical career.

Amy said: "The first time I heard Dionne sing, I couldn't believe what I was hearing, such an amazing voice from such a young cat.

"She's so much better than I was at her age. I'm just so proud of her."

Amy named her label Lioness Records. She explained that her grandmother, Tituba, had given her a necklace bearing a pendant featuring a lioness, and it was her way of paying tribute to a woman she described as "my best friend … the sweetest, strongest, most amazing person I've ever met."

By October, the debut album was complete. Amy featured as part of the backing band on a 12-song record of soul covers called "Introducing Dionne Bromfield."

Tracks included a version of "Ain't No Mountain High Enough", "My Boy Lollipop" and "Mama Said".

Following in her godmother's footsteps, Dionne was a pupil at the Sylvia Young School. She was also following Amy's example in starting to write her own material, with Amy encouraging her to draw from her own life experiences.

Amy enjoyed being a part of something new and exciting, without wanting to take away the limelight from Dionne. She also knew she could open doors for her goddaughter.

"Dionne is young but she has more potential than any girl I've ever seen," she said. "I know she's got an advantage by knowing me but I'd put her in a room against anyone and she'd do the business."

The first sight the public had of what they were working on was when the pair filmed themselves singing a cover of Alicia Keys' "If I Ain't Got You", posting it on YouTube. In September 2009 they performed together at the Prince's Trust End of the Summer Ball. In between, Amy paid for Dionne to travel to Los Angeles for an intensive 10-day singing course.

The release date for the album was set for October, and to promote the disc Dionne performed lead single "Mama Said" – a cover of the Shirelles' 1960s hit – with Amy as backing singer, on British TV show *Strictly Come Dancing*.

The album peaked at No. 33 in the UK album charts, pleasing both Amy and Dionne, who started writing material for a follow-up almost immediately.

When the second album, "Good for the Soul", was released on July 4 2011, 11 of the 14 tracks were written or co-written by Dionne.

To promote the album, Dionne performed with The Wanted at London's Roundhouse on July 20, with Amy joining her on stage. Three days later, Amy was dead.

HEALTH AND WEALTH

On the back of the continued success of "Back To Black", Amy had built up a personal fortune of around $15million by mid-2008 – she was tied for 10th in a British listing of wealthy musicians under age 30.

A year later, her wealth was reported to be down to half that figure. But money was not a problem; she was in demand. It was reported that she earned around $1.5m singing at two private parties during Paris Fashion Week, and another $1.5 million performing at a Moscow Art Gallery for Russian oligarch Roman Abramovich.

It was clear, with Amy not having signed a pre-nuptial agreement with Blake, that her divorce could be costly.

The fact that, ultimately, he told her wanted nothing may have changed the public's perception of him. One newspaper had described him as "the most reviled man in Britain", but it was clear that he genuinely loved Amy deeply and was not simply a gold-digger.

To some, the fact that Blake had broken out of rehab to see Amy, knowing that it would mean he was sent back to finish his prison sentence, had seemed the ultimate romantic gesture.

Mitch, however, saw things differently. He said: "He went to Amy's room and there was a setback. I was incandescent – someone who wanted to get clean reunited with her junkie husband."

Mitch had not been overly critical of his son-in-law while there was still a chance of the couple reconciling. Once Blake had filed for divorce, though, and Amy told her father she wanted out, he felt able to be more forthright.

He said: "When this does go to court, we're not going to give him anything.

"How can he expect any money? He's a convicted liar, a convicted violent criminal, but there he is trying to convince people that butter wouldn't melt in his mouth.

"I am not saying that he forced Class A drugs down Amy's throat, but now he wants us to believe that he begged her to stop. It's madness."

Georgette Fielder-Civil, for her part, said she was "relieved" the marriage was over.

While Blake served out the rest of his sentence, Amy got on with her recovery.

The fact that her husband had been in jail for so long had not denied her access to drugs. According to Mitch, "people were even throwing drugs over the fence and up to her window for her. Until we brought in our own security, we were finding it a difficult situation to resolve."

It had taken her a long time to get there, but she was later to say that, in the end, giving up the drugs had been easy. "I literally woke up one day and was like, 'I don't want to do this any more.'"

Now drug-free, she was compensating by drinking more.

St Lucia meant she was away from the bad influences in her life, but there was an inexhaustible supply of Jack Daniel's and Coke – Amy's favorite drink.

Janis said her daughter was "in denial all the time." She said: "She probably feels trapped, her body is trapping her. But I know with addiction you do not have the choice because the substance itself directs you. I want to say to her - 'Amy, what are you doing? Don't you know what you're doing?'"

Mitch admitted: "I think potentially she could have a drink problem as addicts tend to replace one addiction with another.

"But she tells me it's something which she will stop – and I believe her. She did it with drugs, so she can do it with alcohol."

He added: "She is a recovering addict and we are a million miles from being cured, but we are getting close to a resolution where she can live her life in a dignified and controlled manner.

"Her security are very astute, they know who to look out for and the signs.

"They even remove her physically from dangerous situations. Saying that, they are not her jailers, and as much as I want to say to Amy: 'Don't drink!', you can't."

Mitch was out in St Lucia while Daphne Barak filmed *"Saving Amy"*, which would later be shown on Channel 4 in the UK. Off-camera, he told her he thought the important thing was that she was off drugs.

He said: "Who would believe, six months ago, that we'd be at this stage? That she'd be walking, laughing, hosting dinner for you, singing? It's amazing . . . My daughter seems happy. "

Mitch and Janis were delighted that Amy had finally kicked her crack cocaine habit, and convinced she would stay drug-free.

Her alcohol consumption, though, was not the only thing concerning them. They both realized that she might be unable to give up Blake.

Georgette insisted to the media that her son wanted nothing more to do with Amy, and the divorce duly went ahead in July 2009. At a hearing lasting less than two minutes, Blake was granted a full divorce on the grounds of Amy's admitted adultery.

If Blake's mother hoped that would be the end of the story, she was to be disappointed. Within a few weeks of the divorce, he was to tell Amy he wanted to get back together with her.

Janis admitted Amy had told her she still loved Blake, but that her daughter had not gone into details because "[She] knows what we think of Blake so I suppose she's hiding it."

Janis said: "She knows he's bad for her. Who knows what will happen?"

"I'm not sure how much more I could go through," she admitted.

She was to tell Barak more about how she felt about Blake. Janis said: "When she was on tour with him, he just followed her round like a lap dog and he did nothing. So it's a case that he's earned his nobody position because he is a nobody."

She added: "Blake called me mummy and it was like you could have stuck a knife in my belly. 'Mummy?'"

Even though Amy spent the majority of the first half of 2009 on St Lucia, relaxing and apparently working on new material, she was again frustrating her label, Island.

They knew she had taken her mobile recording equipment with her to the Caribbean, but they were hearing little to encourage them to think her new album would be ready anytime soon.

Island executives hoped that, when Amy agreed to play at a party to celebrate the label's 50th birthday in late May, that they might hear some new songs. But Amy changed her mind and pulled out.

Even when Amy did manage to hold it together enough to perform for an audience, her appearances – like that at the Grammys in 2008 – were rarely reviewed independent of her personal problems.

Singer Natalie Cole, who had battled her own demons, said it had been a mistake to expose her to the public while she was trying to kick drugs. She said: "I just don't get it. What more can we do other than everybody needs to grow up? Hollywood needs to grow up and stop glorifying this kind of behaviour and thinking it's cute."

Jody Rosen, writing on *Slate* after the Grammys performance, said it had "offered hope that she may finally be putting her worst self-destructive habits behind her. But it was also a reminder that, to a great degree, self-destruction is her muse."

With prescience, the article continued: "The most obvious influence on her drawling, raspy vocal style is Billie Holiday, pop's supreme emotional masochist, who, by the way, drank and doped herself to death."

It was hard for Amy to stay out of the headlines, despite spending so much time out of the country.

In March she was arrested and charged with assault, over the alleged incident at the Prince's Trust ball the previous September.

When the case came to court, Amy pleaded not guilty of punching a woman in the eye, saying that she had simply pushed the woman away because she was scared. The judge, to her relief, found her not guilty.

Later in the year, though, she faced another assault charge as well as one of disorderly behaviour. She had been charged over an incident involving a manager at the Milton Keynes Theatre.

Prosecutors told the court Amy had drunk five vodka and cokes before the manager, who had received complaints about her behaviour from other members of the audience, suggested she might be better to switch to water.

The court heard Amy had sworn at him, and though she then apologised he asked her to leave the theatre. The prosecution told how she had then grabbed his hair and asked him: "Who the fuck do you think you are?"

Evidently he thought he was someone entitled to much greater respect. He complained to police, and ultimately Amy was given a two-year conditional discharge as well as having to pay £185 (approx. $248) in costs and compensation.

FINAL DAYS

When Amy invited Mitch to join her in St Lucia, he hoped it would be a relaxing holiday, a chance to spend quality time with his daughter.

Yet again, though, he found himself acting as her guardian. She was drinking very heavily, and none of her entourage had the courage to confront her about it. "I don't think I'll come here again," he told Daphne Barak.

When Daphne arrived on the island to film her, she found him in a bleak mood. Her addiction was like an egg timer; eventually all the sand had disappeared from her drug habit, but it was just in a different place.

Mitch said: "I can't approve of her addiction and drinking. She should know that."

The next day his frustrations were evident. He told Daphne: "She said to me today, 'Dad, thank you for pulling me out of drugs', and I said to her, 'But you are the one who decided to pull out. You can do it again and stop drinking'."

He added: "She has progressed so much. But now, if it's alcohol instead of hard drugs — I don't think I can go through the same thing again. I've decided to distance myself, and whatever happens, happens. It's her life. It's her career. It's her decision."

Maybe he was being serious, but tough love was hard to administer. Amy was a huge international star who had always ploughed her own furrow, but she was also still his little girl.

While being filmed for the documentary, she put on the song "Daddy's Home." Daphne wrote in her diary. "Mitch's eyes fill with tears. Amy is now sitting on the drums and beating out the rhythm: 'Dad, dad, come here . . .' She motions to Mitch and gives him her seat at the drums. As he begins to drum, she picks up a guitar and accompanies him.

"At the end of the song, she runs to him and gives him a kiss on the lips. Mitch is still looking very emotional."

Later, when she cuts her leg, she goes straight to sit on her father's lap.

Amy was to tell Chris Willman that it was difficult for her to refuse drinks when her entourage bought them for her.

She said sometimes she would tell them she was not drinking and, if they asked why, "I always say that I'm on antibiotics. Because I'm ashamed to just go, "You know, I'm just not drinking." I have to say that I'm on a course of medication, because I feel ashamed (about abstaining)."

One of the last thing Daphne noticed on her trip was Amy sucking her thumb. Mitch went over to her and silently pulled it out of her mouth.

Mitch told *the Times* that, having spoken to counsellors and therapists, he genuinely felt Amy's problem "isn't an addiction; it's just that she drinks too much every now and again. It's not alcoholism."

In the same piece, though, he was quoted as admitting: "Delusion is part of the protection … you cling onto little things; little things become massive triumphs."

He said that, while she clearly had addictive tendencies, sometimes they could be channelled positively. "There are also positive addictions, like her gym work," he said. "She's got the physiology – if that's the right word – of, like, an Olympic athlete. The doctor who saw me last week said: 'She could go into the Olympics, she's so fit.'"

It is no secret that Amy Winehouse had emotional and psychological disorders which undoubtedly contributed to her drug use. Diagnosed as having Manic-Depressive Illness (also known as Bipolar Disorder) she did what 30 to 60 percent of its sufferers do - turn to alcohol and/or drugs to make the extreme mood swings caused by the illness easier to bear.

Manic-Depressive Illness is characterized by extreme mood swings which alternate between manic episodes and depressive episodes. Some symptoms of depressive episodes are: anxiety, sadness, irritability, hopelessness, suicidal ideation. Some symptoms of manic episodes are: insomnia, inability to concentrate, pressured speech, and racing thoughts. The intensity of such mood swings take not only an emotional toll on the sufferer, but may result in physical illness as well.

At the same time, it is interesting that Bipolar Disorder and creativity are linked, which suggests the chemical imbalance which causes drastic mood swings also results in higher forms of abstract thinking - and, it is this abstract way of thinking which often results in tangible artistic results.

Beethoven, Van Gogh, Robin Williams, Kurt Cobain, Jimi Hendrix, Sylvia Plath, Mark Twain, Goethe, Virginia Woolf, Vivien Leigh, Edgar Allen Poe, and Lord Byron are just a few examples of creative geniuses who were plagued with Manic-Depressive Illness!

While the upside of manic episodes is increased mental productivity, the downside is that extreme mood swings often leave its bearers with a desire to self-medicate in order to stabilize, though this never tends to work. Sleeping pills during bouts of insomnia, pain killers during bouts of depression (depression may cause physical pain in the body) - when one's judgment is off balance, the consequences of not following doctors' orders show themselves as spending sprees, sexual promiscuity due to an increased sex drive, and during moments of dark depression, suicidal tendencies.

It has been reported that one out of every three patients diagnosed with Bipolar Disorder will attempt suicide or complete it.

Knowing this about Manic-Depressive Illness, it is evident Amy had demons of her own to contend with outside of her intense relationships with lovers. To call her just a drug addict or a drunk would be unfair. Amy was a daughter and sister, a friend, an artist, a mentor. She was a young woman whose love of art and beauty resulted in artistic endeavors which shall be remembered for all time. She was a soul who touched hearts, who moved the world with her passionate voice. Amy was, above all, a complex individual.

Bipolar Disorder is much more common than most people believe. In the USA, there are around 5.7 million people with the condition, while the number in the UK is almost 750,000. The authors hope that, with a little understanding and a great deal of compassion, we can each make a difference so that tragedies like Amy's don't happen again.

Amy's excessive drinking sometimes led to intolerable behaviour. When she first got to St Lucia she stayed in a hotel but there were complaints and she quickly moved into a private chalet.

Former government spokesman Jeff Fedee was not impressed, calling her a "tattooed reptile" who was a bad influence on the youth of St Lucia.

She wanted to counter that perception, and agreed to play at the island's annual jazz festival. But in the end she turned up late, drunk and "too emotional" to sing.

Her label hoped against hope that she could stay sober long enough to put together some songs worthy of being released.

The combined bill for her and entourage – which included friends, general hangers-on and half a dozen minders – topped £500,000, but that would have been small change if Amy had managed to record a third album.

Brian Rose, commercial director of her US label Universal, flew out to St Lucia to see if Amy had been able to write anything new since they told her in March, having listened to her initial demos, that she needed to start again. But having locked herself in the studio for hours at a time to record those demos, she was so discouraged at Universal's reaction she virtually stopped writing.

Producer Salaam Remi flew in to see her and see if he could help, but she was too drunk to meet him.

Though at times it fueled her excesses, the alcohol could also bring on morose moods. The fact that she and Blake had been to St Lucia for their honeymoon was not lost on her, and the *Daily Mail* reported she told one guest "We're still in love, though. I do love him."

By this time, though, Blake had moved on. Fresh out of prison, he revealed girlfriend Gileen Morris, who he had met in rehab the previous year, was expecting their baby. Gileen was to tell the media that, initially, she had wanted to have an abortion but Blake talked her out of it and insisted he would stand by her.

Amy told the guest: "He's having a baby now and I'm so, so happy." That happiness didn't seem reflected in the title of the song the Mail reported she had written about it – "Ultimate Betrayal".

Whether it was at Universal's request or that Amy just wanted to return to London, the St Lucia party broke up not long after she was hospitalised on the island, suffering from chest pains.

It was just one of the times during the final three years of her life that Amy would need hospital treatment, but every time her family – and her fans – hoped the interventions had helped they were to prove mere false dawns.

Repeated suggestions through the media that a new album was on its way were treated with increasing amounts of scepticism.

Even though there were no signs of new releases, the papers had not become bored with Amy.

Journalist Paul Willis wrote on *CNN's* website, after Amy's death, that the media's "bad-taste documenting of her downward spiral bordered on cruelty … columnists wrung their hands in false concern at the plight of 'poor Amy,' even as their editors turned the star's descent into a gruesome public spectacle."

Indeed, she was bothered by the paparazzi enough to seek an injunction preventing them from following her within 100 metres of her home.

She had no powers to stop them from turning up wherever she drank or dined, though. If she had hoped to keep a reunion with Blake in March 2010 secret it was in vain, as photographers snapped the pair kissing after eating tapas at her regular haunt, Jamon Jamon.

The following month, the papers were reporting that the couple were ready to make a fresh start. They were pictured hand in hand outside the Jazz After Dark bar, where they had celebrated Blake's 28th birthday.

Club owner Sam Shaker told *People* magazine: "They are in love with each other. If people would not interfere with all their life, they are amazing together. They are happy together, and that's all that matters to me."

Their respective parents were horrified by the reports, particularly in the light of earlier stories that Blake had got engaged to another woman he had met in rehab, Sarah Aspin.

It came as a relief all round when, a couple of months later, Amy stepped out with a new man.

Reg Traviss, a singer and film maker, who had directed the British film *Psychosis*, were pictured hand in hand out shopping in central London.

To Mitch, Reg was entirely suitable as a prospective son-in-law. He told reporters: "I am happy she's got a new boyfriend, I am happy she's moving on with her life. He's a normal bloke, very nice."

It was a fatherly reaction, and though Mitch and Janis were very aware of their daughter as a commercial artist – the pair administered her earnings – a part of Mitch would only ever see her as a normal woman with normal desires.

Asked what he would wish for her, he said: "I would want her to be is as she is – a normal, lovely person with a loving family – and to find a man … a person she loves and who loves her and who cherishes her and wants to have children with her.

"I do care about her career, but it's secondary. In other words, I'd prefer it if she had a normal life being a normal person, but she's not."

It seemed, though, that however well Amy and Blake did in dealing with their drink and drug addictions, their efforts to go cold turkey and wean themselves off each other would never be successful.

Georgette, under pressure to defend her son after Amy's death, revealed that in 2010 he had received a letter from his ex-wife. "Please God, hopefully, I'd have your baby kicking to come out of me," she wrote. "Fix me! Let me fix you! We've always looked after each other, ALWAYS."

As much as some feel Blake is to blame for Amy's descent into drugs, the fact remains that Amy was at one time diagnosed as Manic Depressive, which is an illness which sometimes drives its sufferers to self-medicate. It is important to note that without anyone else's help, Amy's own personal circumstances were sufficient enough to explain the some of the driving forces behind her addictions.

As destructive as Amy and Blake were when together, it was apparent they loved one another body and soul. It was evident they were soul mates.

Reg was to say that he and Amy were happy, and talking about getting married before the end of 2011.

Blake convinced Sarah he was over his ex-wife, and the couple would go on to have a baby together.

Not long before Amy died, though, Sarah was telling *The Sun* that Blake was still getting text messages from her. She said: "I've had enough of her thinking she can click her fingers and get him back whenever she wants.

"She phones him when she is really out of it and her texts are even signed off 'your wife.'"

Friends knew that, in her usually inebriated state, Amy didn't always mean what she said. So it didn't come as a major surprise to Mark that his fall-out with her over their initial meeting to discuss a third album, was not the last he heard of her.

She contacted him later to make up, and Mark revealed after Amy's death that she had written and recorded three songs she hoped would be included on the forthcoming James Bond film.

"To have one of her songs used in the next film would be the perfect memorial to her," Mark said.

He said Amy had written three more songs over the previous year, called 'The Walther Project', 'Revenge Alone' and 'You're The Man,' and recorded in his studio.

"They were really a work in progress but she'd laid down the vocals and had guitar and drums as an outline. It wouldn't take much to tighten it up into a finished product," he added.

The final attempt Amy would make to come back to recording or performing came in June 2011. That night, her family and friends were out in force at a secret gig she played at the 100 Club on Oxford Street.

Mitch was to describe her mood then as "the happiest she has been for years … her voice was good, her wit and timing were perfect."

If that were the final image her fans had of her, it would have helped them remember their heroine as ending her life in happiness.

Sadly, a few days after playing in London, Amy flew to Belgrade to play the first date on her European tour.

Her spokesman said that she had completed an assessment at the Priory Clinic, and was "now looking forward to playing shows around Europe this summer and is raring to go.

"She would like to send a huge thanks to a her fans for the messages of support she has received over the last week and can't wait to see them."

In an attempt to keep her relatively sober, her management had banned alcohol from the entire floor of the hotel where she was staying. It would be in vain.

A backing musician, Ana Zeo Kida, told *The Sun* she only appeared under duress – a claim her management would deny.

Kida said: "Four British bodyguards simply pushed her to step up on stage. She did not want to and was making a scene trying to escape them. It was distressing to see; she obviously needed help."

Late on stage, clearly heavily drunk, she slurred her way through a number of songs without being able to complete any of them.

One fan, who said he had spent his entire weekly salary on the concert ticket, said: "the organisers should have canceed it to let us, her fans, remember the real Amy."

Defence minister Dragan Sutanovac said on his *Facebook* page: "Amy's concert was a shame and a huge disappointment.

"She is far from being a queen. She's more like a patient of a rehabilitation clinic for drugs and an alcohol addict. She needs serious medical assistance."

The 20,000 fans, who had cheered her on, booed her off. They would have no idea that in less than two months Amy would be dead.

ALONE AT THE END

On July 22, 2011, Amy went for a routine appointment with her family doctor. Afterwards, she went home and played the drums into the early hours.

As was usual, her live-in security guard Andrew Morris kept guard outside the front door of her house. Other than remind her at around 2am to keep the noise down, he had no contact with Amy that night.

When he went to check on her at 10am, he saw her apparently asleep. He heard nothing more from her, so at around three o'clock in the afternoon he went in to check again.

He realized that Amy had died.

Reliving the moment he discovered her body, he said: "When I went in the room she was lying on the bed in the same position from 10am. I was immediately concerned, went over and checked to see if she was OK. I checked on her and realized she wasn't breathing and had no pulse so called the emergency services."

When paramedics arrived at the apartment, they confirmed that Amy had died.

Within an hour of the news being released to the media, camera crews appeared in front of her house and fans gathered to pay their respects, though the street was soon cordoned off by the police as forensic investigators entered the North London flat.

There was shock around the world as the news broke on every major news organisation, and quickly the tributes poured in.

Universal released a statement saying "We are deeply saddened at the sudden loss of such a gifted musician, artist and performer."

Keith Urban, who had successfully fought battles with drink and drugs, said his "heart really breaks" for Amy's family, "because there's only so much you can do."

He explained: "There does come a point where you have to pull away or detach with love as they say because otherwise the entire ship is going to go down, and you can't help someone who doesn't want help."

Rihanna tweeted:
"I am genuinely heartbroken about this, dear Amy." Another tweet, from Demi Moore, said: "Truly sad news about Amy Winehouse. My heart goes out to her family. May her troubled soul find peace."

Actor Russell Brand wrote on his blog: "We have lost a beautiful and talented woman to this disease. Not all addicts have Amy's incredible talent. Or Kurt's or Jimi's or Janis's, some people just get the affliction.

"All we can do is adapt the way we view this condition, not as a crime or a romantic affectation but as a disease that will kill. We need to review the way society treats addicts, not as criminals but as sick people in need of care."

British singer Olly Murs said: "It's shocking, such an awful thing to happen to such a great artist."

Rapper MIA posted a tribute song, "27" on Amy's Soundcloud page within 24 hours of hearing of her death.

Two of her backing singers, brothers Heshima and Zalon Thompson, revealed they were also planning a musical tribute to Amy.

Heshima told the BBC, "Amy was just so real, she was so honest and she was so open. You didn't really have to wonder what she was thinking - you pretty much knew."

Zalon added: "She didn't like the glitz and glam - she hated it. So many people wanted to work with her and she wasn't about that, she wasn't about the money, she was pure about music."

Jamiroquai said on *Facebook*: "Amy Winehouse was a true British talent, with a natural gift for Jazz and Soul. She will be missed by everyone who has a passion for music with raw emotion at it's heart. We dedicated 'High Times' to Amy at last night's gig in tribute to her. We'll miss you, Amy x."

Kurt Cobain's widow Courtney Love, took time out from a concert in Russia to talk about the friend she tried to counsel twice about her demons: "I'm not even going to say, "Waste of glorious sublime talent."

Simon Vozick-Levinson, associate editor of *Rolling Stone* magazine, said of her, "We never quite heard a voice that was quite like that. She really put her own very unique spin on the influences she drew on."

Former *Girls Aloud* singer Kerry Katona said: "I feel so sad about Amy and my heart goes out to all her friends, her family, her fans and everyone who knew and loved her," but added: "If you mess with drugs, you've got to deal with the consequences before it's too late."

American TV anchor Piers Morgan said the people who were "making money out of her" in the end "let her down" by not being with her at the end. He said: "Of course it's down to Amy Winehouse, but this kid was this big with the most incredible talent."

Tony Bennett, the last person to work with Amy, *told Us Weekly* she was "an extraordinary musician with a rare intuition as a vocalist. She was a lovely and intelligent person."

He added: "Of all the contemporary artists I've worked with, she has the most natural jazz voice. Her phrasing and tone – she's got it."

Cee Lo Green revealed he and Amy had been planning to work together, having been introduced through mutual friend Salaam Remi. He said: "I could listen to her and she registered to me as the real thing... It's so untimely and unfortunate. What a loss. Music has lost a daughter."

Salaam said: "At the end, she was a real person. She had a huge heart."

He added: "We'd be working for hours and she would have everybody in the room snickering. She always had a joke. You could hear a lot of that in her lyrics, she could be sarcastic and she was extremely witty ... but more than anything else she was a real person, an individual artist."

Kelly Osborne, a close friend of Amy, was to wear her hair in a beehive in her honour when she attended the funeral. After hearing the news of her death, she tweeted, "I cant even breath [sic] right my now im crying so hard i just lost 1 of my best friends. i love you forever Amy & will never forget the real you!"

Mark tweeted, "she was my musical soulmate & like a sister to me. this is one of the saddest days of my life."

He honoured Amy several days after her death, by playing a series of her tracks at the Greenwich Summer Sessions in London.

Contactmusic quoted him as telling the crowd: "I went to her service yesterday and a Rabbi said 'a person's life is measured in deeds, not years'; hers was pretty f**king special.'

"I'm not getting emotional or morbid but it's nice to share this moment with people who appreciate good music. Amy Winehouse was a genius and has made more brilliant music than I'll ever make," he added.

Amy's funeral took place on July 26, three days after death, at Edgwarebury Lane cemetery in North London, with the private service being led by Rabbi Frank Hellner.

Mitch delivered the eulogy, saying: "Goodnight, my angel, sleep tight. Mummy and Daddy love you ever so much.

She was cremated at Golders Green Crematorium, her ashes placed next to those of her grandmother Cynthia.

After her death, Reg was described by some news sources as "her on-off boyfriend", with the pair's exact status unclear. But Reg told the Sun they had been planning their wedding.

He said: "Amy kept trying to decide what to wear. She had laid out her dresses to make up her mind. She was really looking forward to it."

Reg added: "She has been full of life and so upbeat recently, exercising everyday and doing yoga. This terrible thing that happened is like an accident.

"The last three days have been hell. We have suffered a terrible untimely loss and want peace now.

"I can't describe what I am going through and I want to thank so much all of the people who have paid their respects and who are mourning the loss of Amy, such a beautiful, brilliant person and my dear love. I have lost my darling who I loved very much."

He told *The Sun*: "We were talking on Friday and I was going to go over, because I was finishing up late at work — but I couldn't get hold of her, so I thought she must have fallen asleep. I sat in and read a book, still no call back. Met some friends and had a drink. Still no call, or anything. So I went home, sent her a text, saying I was staying up watching a DVD and told her to call as soon as she woke up. If I'd gone over there, I'd have woken her up, we'd have sat up all night watching films."

He remembered how he had heard the news. He said he had noticed there had been a missed call from Andrew Morris but did not immediately ring the security guard back.

"When I got to the office I rang and spoke to the security guy. He just said, 'Reg. Something terrible has happened'. You could tell in his voice. He said, ;You better get here straight away'. And that was it. I dropped everything and went."

What he discovered was that his fiancee was dead. He said: "It was like everything stopped, like I'd stepped into another reality — a parallel dimension where everything is the same but something is fundamentally wrong.

"You are trying to make sense of it. Keeping yourself together because you know now nothing is going to be the same again, ever."

He went on : "If there was a steady build-up, then you are at least in a mindset where you are expecting the next thing to happen. But this was very much someone who was completely normal, happy, healthy, talking about the future. When she went, you could essentially say we were in mid-conversation."

At her funeral, Mitch said of Reg: "He helped her with her problems, and Amy was looking forward to their future together."

It must have been galling to Sarah Aspin that she was the means Blake chose to pass on his own reaction.

Perhaps it says much of Blake's ability to dominate relationships, that he could persuade his fiancé to read out the words he had written about his ex-wife. But Blake had little choice, having begun a 32-month sentence for burglary and firearm possession the previous month.

"I will never ever again feel the love I felt for her," he said. "Everybody who knew me and knew Amy knew the depth of our love.

"I can't believe she's dead. My tears will never dry."

Sarah said Blake was "devastated and shattered" by the news.

She told The Sun: "I just couldn't console him. He was in total shock."

Calling Fielder-Civil and Winehouse "soul mates," Sarah added that "they couldn't live with each other, and they couldn't live without each other.

"It's hard for me knowing he still loved her, but I do understand."

Blake's birth father, Larry Fielder, told TMZ that, when Sarah visited him after learning of Amy's death, all he did was cry inconsolably.

Though some may have felt deep sympathy for Blake, others clearly were left feeling he was partly to blame for Amy's death.

His mother, Georgette, told reporters: "I am not asking anyone to say "poor Blake" — he made his choices and he has to live with them.

"I'm not trying to defend his behaviour and I know him for what he is: he's an addict and he has done some terrible things.

"He feels enormous grief and responsibility for some of the things that have happened, as well he should.

"But I also think he's been made the fall guy for what happened to Amy, when the truth is, in fact, far more complicated."

Georgette added: "Amy frequently said that the only person who could fix her was Blake. She spoke to Blake the whole time before she died.

"Friends of Blake's have told me that she telephoned him in prison the day before she died and asked if he could arrange for a visiting order."

Georgette said the couple were always ringing each other and that, irrespective of being engaged to Sarah, Blake "always wanted her back." She added: "She couldn't walk away from him and he couldn't walk away from her."

She went on: "Yes, they were passionate, and they fought, but they were also just a young couple deeply in love and I have lots of ordinary memories which I treasure."

Blake's mother blamed Mitch, who she said Amy felt did not give the couple "any room to breathe", for preventing their marriage from working.

Like Mitch, though, she seized on the smallest signs of encouragement and continued to believe her child could win a battle against addiction. Giles, her husband and Blake's stepfather, decided he had had enough and walked out in 2009.

She said when she found out Amy had died, "I felt very very sad. It was difficult to absorb that she was gone for ever."

From sadness at her death, Georgette's mind had quickly turned to concern for her son. She said: "Blake will kill himself. He won't make it without her. He will be devastated, totally and utterly devastated.

"He'll go straight back to self-harming. I'll have to ring the prison and he'll have to be put on watch."

Writing in the *Guardian* in the UK, columnist Deborah Orr wrote: "People don't really believe that alcohol is deadly to the addict. 'Drug addict' is a fearful term. 'Alcoholic' is quite often used capriciously, to denote that a person drinks a lot. But 'an alcoholic' is just a particular subset of drug addict, addicted to a particular drug. Alcohol's legality does not make it any more safe for people who have the illness."

The fact that Blake couldn't be at the funeral was no doubt a consolation to Amy's family. It was not that Mitch wanted to specifically point to finger of blame at him, but that his presence would have seemed inappropriate. Mitch told *the Sun* that he blamed Blake for "starting her on the road to hard drugs," but added: "Her death was a horrible accident. It was her responsibility. She was told that if she detoxed without medical intervention, this whole thing could happen."

Mitch wrote in a letter: "Amy was the greatest daughter, family member and friend you could ever have. Knowing she wasn't depressed, knowing she passed away, knowing she passed away happy, it makes us all feel better."

He also wrote: "When somebody is an addict they have to deal with it in their own way. The only way that the family can help is to be there to love and support them."

He told fans gathered outsider her house: "Amy was about one thing, and that was love. Her whole life was devoted to her family and her friends, and to you guys as well."

Though he had been in the USA when his daughter died, Mitch said they had spoken at least three times every day.

Mitch said his daughter had not drunk in three weeks because she had told him: "Dad I've had enough, I can't stand the look on your and the family's faces anymore."

However, with the post mortem being inconclusive, it was three months before the actual cause of death was determined at the inquest.

Mitch had been right to state that Amy had been teetotal for three weeks, but toxicology tests showed that what she had consumed on the night of her death had poisoned her.

London coroner Suzanne Greenway said: "She had consumed sufficient alcohol at 416mg per decilitre (of blood) and the unintended consequence of such potentially fatal levels was her sudden and unexpected death."

The pathologist who gave evidence said 350mg was considered a fatal dose. At that level, the doctor said, Amy could have stopped breathing and slipped into a coma before dying.

Police recovered three bottles of vodka from her flat, two large and one small. There were no traces of drugs in her system, and her vital organs were in good health.

Her family doctor, Dr Christina Romete, who had been treating her for several years, said she saw Amy the night before she died and described her as a little drunk but coherent.

She said: "The advice I had given to Amy over a long period of time was verbal and in written form about all the effects alcohol can have on the system, including respiratory depression and death, heart problems, fertility problems and liver problems.

"She had her own way and was very determined to do everything her own way," said Dr Romete. "Including any form of therapy. She had very strict views. She was looking forward to the future."

The Winehouse family issued a joint statement, saying: "It is some relief to finally find out what happened to Amy. We understand there was alcohol in her system when she passed away - it is likely a build-up of alcohol in her system over a number of days.

"The court heard that Amy was battling hard to conquer her problems with alcohol and it is a source of great pain to us that she could not win in time."

AMY'S LEGACY

When Amy burst onto the music scene, one of the most common questions journalists would ask was who had influenced her.

After she died, the question was turned on its head – which other artists had Amy most influenced? Among those who were quick to cite her as an inspiration were Lady Gaga and Adele.

Lady Gaga tweeted: "Amy changed pop music forever, I remember knowing there was hope, and feeling not alone because of her. She lived jazz, she lived the blues."

She added: "I really couldn't speak for, like, 48 hours straight. I was in such shock. I don't think Amy needed to learn any lessons. I think the lesson was for the world to be kinder to the superstar. Everybody was so hard on her, and everything that I knew about her was that she was the most lovely and kind woman."

Adele said: "Amy paved the way for artists like me and made people excited about British music again whilst being fearlessly hilarious and blase about the whole thing.

"I don't think she ever realized just how brilliant she was and how important she is, but that just makes her even more charming.

"Although I'm incredibly sad about Amy passing I'm also reminded of how immensely proud of her I* am as well, and grateful to be inspired by her."

The *New York Times* obituary called her "one of the most fascinating figures in pop music since Kurt Cobain." It went on: "Yet in time, the notoriety from Ms. Winehouse's various drug arrests, public meltdowns and ruined concerts overshadowed her talent as a musician, and her career never recovered.

British pop artist Gerald Laing, who had made his name in the 1960s by drawing Brigitte Bardot, opened an exhibition of paintings and drawings documenting Amy's public image in London.

Laing told the *Daily Telegraph*: "These paintings date from a time when each episode in Amy's increasingly complex life was being portrayed by the media.

"My work is concerned with the myth, and portrays her as she appeared to us, the public, via the media. Now that the drama has ended, and all is quiet, I hope it will be seen as a tribute from one artist to another."

Laing's well-intentioned gesture, of donating some of the proceeds from his work to the Amy Winehouse Foundation, unfortunately did little to convince the general public to take the new charity seriously.

It was a natural reaction for Mitch to channel his grief and anger following Amy's death into setting up the foundation in his daughter's death. But he was keen to be as hands-on as possible, and did not seem to be taking good advice as to how to set up the foundation.

The world was listening when, in the weeks after she died, he talked of using the foundation to help others. The charity, though, suffered through a lack of focus and planning.

Mitch said the aim of the foundation was to "help as many young people and children as we can in her name."

But it did not help that, when he discovered that someone had already registered the domain name he wanted, Mitch implied that it was an act of theft. The person who had bought the domain name was ultimately willing to give it up, but unhappy to have been publicly traduced.

Things went from bad to worse. Mitch told the media that the checks he had received made out to "The Amy Winehouse Foundation" were being returned because the domain name did not belong to him. Had he taken 10 minutes to speak to an accountant, he would have found out that the checks themselves were perfectly valid and could be banked if he merely set up an account in that name.

What could have been a marvellous chance to promote the plight of youngsters who face substance abuse issues was badly handled, and the foundation raised far less money in the first few months than might have been expected.

A concert billed as including a "star studded cast", though not featuring any artists that the authors had heard of, was staged a London theatre in November. Even with Mitch performing some of his own repertoire, the event raised just $1000.

One of the problems was that the foundation was far too broad in its aims. Mitch wrote on the website that the foundation had been launched *"to support charitable activities in both the UK and abroad that provide help, support or care for young people, especially those who are*

*in need by reason of ill health, disability, financial
disadvantage or addiction."*

The authors of this book tried a number of times to
contact the foundation, and Mitch personally, to offer
financial support through donating a proportion of the
book's profits.

Eventually, a representative of the foundation sent a
three sentence email saying simply "there is a great deal of
work to be done in setting the Foundation up and putting all
of the necessary systems in place."

It seems clear that, while Mitch's motive in setting up
the foundation to raise money in his daughter's name is
entirely honorable and laudable, in its execution it is falling
woefully short to the point where it is not even able to
accept donations.

The email explained Mitch's unwillingness to even be
interviewed for this biography by saying that he "is currently
writing a book of his own and will therefore not be working
with any other writers."

While the foundation faltered in its aims, though, there
was no shortage of artists who wanted to pay personal
tributes to Amy for the legacy she had left behind. Rapper
Jay-Z credited her with revitalising British music, saying,
"There's a strong push coming out of London right now,
which is great.

"It's been coming ever since I guess Amy (Winehouse). I mean always, but I think Amy, this resurgence was ushered in by Amy."

Keith Caulfield chart manager for *Billboard* wrote that "Because of Amy, or the lack thereof, the marketplace was able to get singers like Adele and Duffy."

Spin magazine were to write that "Amy Winehouse was the *Nirvana* moment for all these women ... they can all be traced back to her in terms of attitude, musical styles or fashion".

Amy's popularity in the USA saw "Back To Black" immediately re-enter the *Billboard* 200 at No.9, with digital sales rising by 2,000 per cent within a week. Amy's tunes were downloaded 111,000 times within seven days, and her radio airplay increased 170 percent.

It was almost possible, in the wake of Amy's death, to forget that she had often been vilified in the Britsh press. In 2008, for example, *NME* magazine nominated her not only in the "Best Solo Artist" category but also for "Villain of the Year." That was also the year she won the "Worst Dressed" award in the magazine.

Glamour magazine named Amy the third worst dressed British Woman, and she was voted the second most hated personality in the United Kingdom in a poll conducted by Marketing magazine.

British *singer* and songwriter Lily Allen told a newspaper: "I know Amy Winehouse very well. And she is very different to what people portray her as being. Yes, she does get out of her mind on drugs sometimes, but she is also a very clever, intelligent, witty, funny person who can hold it together."

When Amy died, it was big news on American TV as well as in the UK. Sales of her music exploded in the following days.

"Back to Black" sold 37,000 copies in a week, and together with her other music it meant she had sold a total of 50,000 albums in seven days. To put it into perspective, up until the week she died she had sold just 44,000 albums in the USA in the previous six months.

The impact her passing had on the world was perhaps best summed up by what happened in social media.

The Independent newspaper in the UK reported that, over the three days following her death, her official *Facebook* page attracted 200,000 users per day.

A company collating social media statistics said that a photo of Amy, put on the page on the day she passed away, had gained more than 130,000 likes in 72 hours, while the total number of people who had liked her official page had passed the three million mark.

After Osama bin Laden was killed, nine per cent of all traffic on Twitter was about him. When Amy died, she was mentioned in more than 11 per cent of tweets.

One of the things the press were quick to latch onto about Amy's death was that she had joined the "27 Club" – musicians who died at age 27.

One of the first members to join the "27 Club" was a ragtime musician by the name of Louis Chauvin who died at the age of 27 in 1908. Chauvin was considered to be one of the finest pianists at the turn of the century. Another member was early blues guitarist Robert Johnson who died at 27 in 1938. A musician of little success, he has since been added to *Rolling Stone's* list of the 100 Best Guitarists of All Time.

Since then, most of the musicians who have died at age 27 have proven to be visionaries with huge followings which have never diminished. It is interesting to note that the highest statistical age of death among musicians does happen to be 27, while the second highest age of death among musicians is age 38.

In general, the "27 Club" refers to a group of musicians who died at age 27 during the years 1969 to 1971. It was at this time Brian Jones of the Rolling Stones was added to the list (died July 3, 1969). From then on the list featured:

- Jimi Hendrix, one of the greatest electric guitarists (died September 18,1970)

- Janis Joplin, a singer/songwriter who is remembered for her powerful vocals (died October 4, 1970)

- Jim Morrison, a poet, musician, and performer (died July 3, 1971)

- Kurt Cobain, singer/songwriter (died April 5, 1994)

- Amy Winehouse singer/songwriter (died July 23, 2011)

Those mentioned are just a few of the most famous names from the list, and it is interesting to note the similarities which these individuals shared at the time of their deaths. They were all 27, all had a reputation for excessive drug and/or alcohol abuse, had emotional/psychological issues, and all of them came from troubled backgrounds with troubled relationships.

While the "27 Club" refers to the musicians who have died at this age, it is also interesting that the origins of the club coincide with superstitions and the astrological journey of the planet Saturn, which takes nearly 30 years to complete its orbit around the sun. Some believe this thirty year transit has a profound effect on each person, especially during the first thirty years of life. That belief is unfounded, while the coincidence of musicians dying at age 27 is statistical in nature.

"LIONESS"

Although Amy had not had finished her third album before she died, it was soon clear from sources close to her that a posthumous CD should be released.

Since Amy died in late July, there was no particular need to rush to reléase the album. A launch date of mid-November would still guarantee plenty of pre-Christmas sales.

It was no surprise that Remi was handed the task of producing the third album, "Lioness: Hidden Treasures".

He told the *Daily Telegraph*: "People have no idea what her actual capacity was. She was so creative, she could flip a song five times, do jazz versions, doo wop, hip hop, trying to find the right arrangement. Musically she was the tops, not just a great singer, she was a great musician, a great writer, and a great producer as well."

Of the 12 tracks on "Lioness", two were demos that Amy had composed with the intention of putting on her third album. There were also unreleased originals, cover versions and alternative versions of familiar tracks.

Remi said: "It's not the album she would have made. But these are things I would like people to know that she did. It makes no sense them sitting on my hard drive wilting away.

Amy had picked out the song titles for the third album, but then had switched direction, according to her producer. Before that album was to be released, she had committed herself to record a jazz disc with a "supergroup" including ?uestlove.

"She had written down everything she wanted to do," Remi told the *Associated Press*.

"She was taking her time with it, and at the end of the day all of her songs are somewhat autobiographical, so she had to live through something, then get out of it and then look back at it to be able to write about it," he said.

"Who knows what will happen in the future with that," he said of the songs she penned.

He said he wanted to release new material from the late singer before others did so.

"Before somebody comes up with some weird song .... this is what it really is," he said. "This is the quality."

Rolling Stone's David Browne wrote: "The album is surprisingly cohesive, polished with background vocals and strings added after her death."

A few days before she died, Winehouse chatted with Remi via Skype, making plans to attend the wedding of Winehouse's former manager Nick Shymansky. "She was really excited," he says. "It was all jokes and talking about what she was going to wear."

Remi never saw her again. "Some kid will pick up an Amy album and say, 'This is really inspiring,' the way she looked up to people like Billie Holiday," he says. "She was inspired by people who passed away before she was born, and she will inspire people who weren't born yet."

The producer did his best with the material, and opted to use some recordings that he made in Amy's first session with him, when she was just 18.

Recalling that first meeting, he said: "Her voice just lit up the room. I thought 'wow!'."

"Her passing hit me pretty hard. I had to get it off my chest, not come back in a year and rehash all the pain I'm feeling now."

The album kicks off with a cover of 1960s doo-wop song "Our Day Will Come", recorded in that first session with Remi in May 2002.

Then comes "Between the Cheats", again recorded by Remi in 2008, and an original ballad versión of "Tears Dry", which had appeared on "Back To Black".

Amy's recording of "Wake Up Alone", the fourth track on the album, is a one-track demo laid down by Paul O'Duffy in March 2006.

The first of the classic covers follows, her rendition – with the Dap Kings – of Carole King's "Will You Still Love Me Tomorrow". Chris Elliott added a string arrangement to the original.

Another versión of "Valerie", this time a slower-tempo rendition recorded in December 2006, leads into her collaboration with American rapper Nas on "Like Smoke".

The next two songs take us right back to the beginning, before the reléase of "Frank". A cover of "The Girl From Ipanema" and the song "Halftime" take the listener through to "Best Friends", with which she opened her live sets during the "Frank" era.

The final track, a heartbreaking versión of Donny Hathaway's classic "A Song for You", was a good way to end the album as it showed fans where she was at, musically, in her post-"Back To Black" days on St Lucia.

The standout single from the disc, though, was "Body & Soul", with Tony Bennett.

Everything about this track was right. As was fitting for a recording that was released on what would have been her 28th birthday. Recorded at the world-famous Abbey Road Studios in London, where the Beatles worked with producer Sir George Martin, it was recorded by Phil Ramone and destined for Bennett's second collaborative album, "Duets Two".

Nicholas Ransbottom, in the *Charleston Gazzette,* wrote of the song: "'Body and Soul' deserves a special mention, as it's the last song Winehouse recorded before her death. It's fitting, then, that she gives the best vocal performance of her life. She and Bennett sound so sincere, friendly and romantic in their singing, and their voices create a velvety lullaby of a love song."

"She got right into the jazz groove, and the record came out beautiful," Bennett told *Rolling Stone.*

It was not a universally popular song, though, and in contrast to the Bennett album – which went straight to no. 1 – the single only reached 87 in the USA and 40 in the UK.

Christopher Loudon, in *Jazz Times* magazine, wrote: The much-ballyhooed unión … at first seems mannered, her desire to emulate Billie Holiday a bit too obvious, but ends in a blaze of fused glory."

Darcus Beese said there were a number of other songs that could have been released on "Lioness", but that Island and Amy's family had insisted that some of them should remain forever unreleased.

Speaking about one track, "Procrastinate", Island boss Ted Cockle told the Guardian: "Everyone who hears [the song] loves it", but Beese said the label had decided it would never be issued.

Mitch told *The Sun* he had wept when he first listened to the album. He said: "I spent so much time chasing after Amy — telling her off — that I never realized what a true genius she was.

"It wasn't until I sat down with the rest of the family and listened to this album that I fully appreciated the breadth of her talent. From jazz standards to hip-hop songs, it took my breath away."

DISCOGRAPHY

STUDIO ALBUMS

"Frank"

Released October 20 2003

Highest chart position (up to November 2011): 3 (UK)

UK chart position: 3

US chart position: 33

Certifications: UK 3 x Platinum, France Gold, Germany Platinum, Switzerland Platinum

"Back To Back"

Released October 4 2006

Highest chart positions: 1 (UK, Austria, France, Germany, Ireland, Netherlands, New Zealand, Switzerland)

US chart position: 2

Certifications: UK 6 x Platinum (standard), 2 x Platinum (deluxe), Australia 3 x Platinum, Germany 6 x Platinum, New Zealand 2 x Platinum, Switzerland 6 x Platinum, US 2 x Platinum

COMPILATION ALBUMS

"Lioness: Hidden Treasures"

Released December 5 2011

EPs

Sessions@AOL:

Released June 1 2004

iTunes Festival, London 2007:

Released August 13 2007

BOX SETS

"Frank/Back To Black":

Released November 24 2008 (4CD box set)

SINGLES

"Stronger Than Me" (from "Frank"):

Released 2003

UK chart position: 71

"Take The Box" (from "Frank"):

Released 2004

UK chart position: 57

"In My Bed/You Sent Me Flying" (from "Frank"):

Released 2004

UK chart position: 60

"Fuck Me Pumps/Help Yourself" (from "Frank"):

Released 2004

UK chart position: 69

"Rehab" (from "Back To Black"):

Released 2006

Highest chart position: 7 (UK)

US chart position: 9

Certifications: NZ Gold, US Platinum, Switzerland Platinum, Denmark Platinum, Belgium Gold, Italy Gold, Spain 2x Platinum

"You Know I'm No Good" (from "Back To Black"):

Released 2007

Highest position: 7 (Switzerland)

UK chart position: 18

US chart position: 77

"Back To Black" (from "Back To Black"):

Released 2007

Highest chart position: 3 (Austria)

UK chart position: 8

"Tears Dry On Their Own" (from "Back To Black"):

Released 2007

Highest position: 16 (UK)

"Love is a Losing Game" (from "Back To Black"):

Released 2007

Highest chart position: 33 (UK)

"Just Friends" (from "Back To Black"):

Released 2008

Did not chart

"Body & Soul" (duet with Tony Bennett)

Released 2011

Highest position: 27 (France)

UK chart position: 40

US chart position: 87

AS FEATURED ARTIST

"Valerie" (Mark Ronson featuring Amy Winehouse)

Released 2007

Highest position: 1 (Netherlands)

UK chart position: 2

"B Boy Baby" (Mutya Buena featuring Amy Winehouse)

Released: 2007

UK chart position: 73

"It's My Party" (Quincy Jones featuring Amy Winehouse)

Released 2010

Did not chart

OTHER CHARTED SONGS

"Valerie" (solo Live Lounge version)

Released 2007

Highest chart position: 33 (Ireland)

UK chart position: 37

"Cupid"

Released 2008

Highest chart position: 49 (Switzerland)

UK chart position: Did not chart

VIDEO ALBUMS

"I Told You I Was Trouble: Live in London"

Released November 5 2007

Made in the USA
Charleston, SC
14 December 2011